B. W. (Basil William) Maturin

Some Principles and Practices of the Spiritual Life

B. W. (Basil William) Maturin

Some Principles and Practices of the Spiritual Life

ISBN/EAN: 9783744653183

Printed in Europe, USA, Canada, Australia, Japan

Cover: Foto ©Thomas Meinert / pixelio.de

More available books at **www.hansebooks.com**

SOME

PRINCIPLES AND PRACTICES

OF

The Spiritual Life

BY

B. W. MATURIN

MISSION PRIEST OF THE SOCIETY OF S. JOHN THE EVANGELIST
OXFORD

THIRD EDITION

LONGMANS, GREEN, AND CO.

LONDON, NEW YORK, AND BOMBAY

1896

TO THE CONGREGATION OF

ST CLEMENT'S, PHILADELPHIA, U.S.A.

IN MEMORY OF

TEN HAPPY YEARS' MINISTRY

AND MANY KINDNESSES RECEIVED FROM THEM

THIS VOLUME IS DEDICATED

CONTENTS.

SOME

PRINCIPLES AND PRACTICES

OF THE

SPIRITUAL LIFE.

———◦◦◦———

I.

THE CHRISTIAN AIM.

BESIDES the general effort which every Christian
must make to do what is right and to keep from
what is wrong, it is important that he should
have some special and definite aim which will
help to keep him from dissipating his strength,
The end of the Christian life is, of course, *holiness*, but holiness is rather an indefinite thing
to beginners, and it may manifest itself in many
forms. And those who would attain to holiness

must begin as they are, with their many sins and imperfections and ignorances, and work on towards an end that becomes clearer as they advance, and yet ever more difficult of attainment. Indeed, they have to work towards an end which at first they cannot see, for only as the eye of the soul becomes purified does it get to see clearly what holiness means, and how imperfect were its first conceptions of it. It is a good thing, therefore, to concentrate our efforts, to be definite in our aim, to set before ourselves clearly some one purpose, some special virtue to strive after, upon the attainment of which we shall have advanced considerably towards holiness of life.

Now there are two kinds of virtues which we may seek after : there are particular virtues which may counteract certain specific evil tendencies of the soul, and help to overcome individual sins ; and the acquirement of these virtues is, of course, essential to the advancement of all. One may need to conquer sloth by diligence, or pride by humility, or irritability by patience ; but this does not necessarily lead the soul to its end; it needs more than this ; one may overcome certain individual sins and never go further, nor even aim at holiness.

There are, therefore, other more comprehensive virtues which involve in their acquisition much more than merely any one virtue or grace, and which lead on definitely and directly to holiness of life; and such virtues cannot be gained, even in any degree, without a very manifest growth in holiness ; for they attack not merely one sin but the root of all the sin that is in us. In proportion as we acquire them, sin loses its hold upon our whole system : its vigour flags ; the old man loses strength because the new man grows stronger ; the sun rises over the whole being, and the ice-bound nature thaws, and all the germs of the new life begin to bud and blossom.

There are some people who seem never to get beyond the attack upon individual sins and the aim after particular virtues. They do not get a large and comprehensive view of the ailments of their nature, or perceive in what its perfection consists: they attack, so to speak, each separate symptom of their disease, but they have never made a diagnosis of their state, and attacked that which is the cause of all these different symptoms. They resemble the man in the Gospel who asked our Lord, 'Which is the great commandment in the law?'[1] as though each commandment stood separate and disconnected from all the others, and as if a person might set himself to keep one perfectly to the neglect of all the others. The observance of the law as a whole seems scarcely to have occurred

[1] S. Matt. xxii. 36.

to him as a possibility, for he did not perceive that the details of the Decalogue were the expression in various relations of one great and comprehensive principle. So our Lord answers him by showing him that the only way to observe them was by striving after the principle which underlay them all. He says : 'You will never be able to keep the commandments if your aim is to observe them one by one The spirit that underlies them all is love ; strive after that, and you will find that in proportion as you gain that all-embracing virtue you are observing all the commandments.'

So, on the other hand, S. James says, 'Whosoever shall keep the whole law, and yet offend in one point, he is guilty of all ' ; [1] that is to say, by the deliberate violation of one of the commandments one shows one's self in antagonism to the spirit and principle of the moral law.

[1] S. James, ii. 10.

Our aim, therefore, should be to strive after
those more comprehensive virtues which involve
the spirit of holiness, and bring in their train a
multitude of graces, though this will of course
necessitate the constant wrestling with individual
sins. But it involves more: it involves a positive rather than a negative life. Its method is
to aim at a spirit which necessarily protects one
from sin. We do not wish to develop a merely
colourless character, of which it can be said that
it does not display any marked or definite faults.
We want to develop a character, on the contrary,
that *is* marked and definite; that shines with
bright virtues; that puts itself forth in action,
strong and vigorous. We have not in any way
got near a definition of God when we say He is
not unjust, or cruel, or evil. God *is* love and
holiness. And it is the same with man: he is
not to be content with eliminating, one after
another, those evident faults that disfigure his

character. He has done nothing towards a holy life till his character can be defined rather in positive than negative terms ; in stating what he *is* rather than what he is not. The wise physician sets himself, not merely to cure one ailment or another, but to build up the constitution with a vigorous health, strong enough to resist the attacks of disease.

And the soul will do this by building up its spiritual life upon principles that undermine all the evil that is in it by developing such virtues as bring it face to face with God, such virtues as strike at the root of sin.

It is possible to set one's self to fight against one's sins, and in the struggle never to get out of one's self, never to get really nearer to God. It is possible, perhaps more than possible ; for the method of struggle sometimes seems to keep people down rather than raise them up. What a difference there is in the whole cha-

racter and religious bearing between one whose
struggle consists merely in an effort not to give
in to any sharp speech and uncharitableness,
and one who with the same fault sets himself
with all his might to gain the love of God, and
of others in and for God.   Such a person
aims at something vastly higher than the mere
victory over his sin ; and even in his failures on
the way we feel that he has far outstripped his
companion who may not fail so badly, but has
not aimed so high.   The one, when he has overcome his fault, may still be no nearer positive
love ; the other is on the way to it long before
his fault is overcome.

Now this is the underlying principle of our
Lord's teaching.   He begins His teaching with
the Beatitudes.   In these He lays down the
great laws of the life of holiness : they are
given, not like the old law, in the form of
prohibitions—' Thou shalt not '—but in the form

of blessings. It is not 'Cursed are the forni-
cators and adulterers,' but 'Blessed are the pure
in heart.' This may seem but another way of
stating the same truth, but we shall see that it
is not; it is the expression of a great principle.
The new law does not merely forbid men to do
what is positively wrong; it begins a step higher
than that; it takes us into that loftier region in
which we are to be set free from the mere curb
of prohibitions by living under the blessings of
active obedience. The old law forbade positive
impurity: 'Thou shalt not commit adultery.'
The new law turns away from the sin, and directs
the soul to God : ' Blessed are the pure in heart :
for they shall see God.' In that vision of God
which this beatitude points the soul to there is
no need to warn against such sin; the soul is
freed from it; it is striving after that which
makes it impossible. Again, the old law said,
'Thou shalt not bear false witness,' and those

who live in its spirit may strive very hard not to slander others. The new law begins on a higher level : it bids men aim at that which makes slander impossible : 'Blessed are the peacemakers : for they shall be called the children of God.' It says, Do not be content with being in the world negatively doing no harm to others; try positively to do good, to make peace, and this as a child of God. The old law forbade covetousness and stealing ; the new turns the whole bent of the soul in another direction ; away from the things of earth to the things of heaven. 'Blessed are the poor in spirit : for theirs is the kingdom of heaven.' One might keep the letter of the eighth and tenth commandments all one's life and never attain to the spirit of the first beatitude. No one could strive after the spirit of this beatitude without being set free, more than free, from all that these commandments prohibit. Living under the principle of the law of prohibitions, one might obey the letter and never develop a character enlarged and enriched by positive and active goodness. One might, as it were, stand on the borderland between right and wrong, not doing positive wrong, and that is all, keeping one's nature under bit and bridle from breaking away into a life of sin, ever conscious of a power of evil within which is ready to assert itself if the rein were loosened. Under the principle of the new law such a state of things is impossible : the soul is not content with restraints ; it has passed into the region of its true development ; it has been shown, not what it is not to do, but what it is to do ; and the line of its development is in direct opposition to that in which its danger lies.

This, then, is the principle of the Christian life : it is positive rather than negative ; it aims at something very much higher than keeping

from definite acts of sin ; it looks upon all laws
of constraint as useless unless they tend to
direct the currents of life towards their true
end.   It does not look upon such laws as an
end in themselves, nor does it consider that by
the mere submitting to the letter of such laws
the soul has fulfilled their purpose.   No ; ' habits
of honesty, habits of prayer, are mere bondages
unless they are helping somehow the produc-
tion of a free, honest, and prayerful nature.
The only object in bandaging and twisting a
man's crooked leg is that some day it may get
a free straightness into it which will make it keep
its true shape when it is set free from bandages ;
if that day is never coming, bandaging is mere
wanton cruelty.   Better take the bandages off
and let it be crooked, if it is getting no inner
straightness, and will be crooked as soon as they
are removed.   So all these commandments and
prohibitions which God lays before us : they

are mere cruelty; they merely torture and worry humanity ; they come to nothing unless within them some free law of inner rectitude is growing up. One looks across God's great moral hospital, sees crooked souls tied up in constraint, and wonders, as one might who looked through a surgeon's ward, behind how many of those bandages an inner life is gathering which some day will ask no binding up, and need nothing but its own liberty to be its law. It is a strange question. Suppose to-morrow all the laws of constraint should be repealed together ; all social penalties, all public restrictions, lifted off together ; nothing left but the last legislation of character : what would become of us ? How just as soon as our bandages were off our unshaped lives would fall into their shapeless-ness ! '

There are thus two regions in which we may live : one on the lowlands, where we ever stand in danger of the penalty of violating the law, in which we are ever conscious of the presence of the law standing over us with its drawn sword in stern warning, in which we are trying not to do wrong; and the other upon the higher plains that breathe with blessings. Those who live there aim at something higher than escape from the curse of breaking the law; they strive after positive holiness; they keep far out of the reach of the curse, within the region of the Beatitudes; they stand no longer tampering with evil, looking at the forbidden fruit and parley-ing with the tempter, arguing as to the terms of the command laid down by God whether it was a distinct prohibition forbidding them to eat or not; they keep well out of the reach of the forbidden tree, filling their lives so full of all that blesses that soon they have forgotten that such a tree exists.

It does indeed produce an entire change in

the whole conception of the Christian life when one passes from under the law of prohibitions to live under the benign influences of the law or the Beatitudes. One ceases merely to strive against particular sins, and begins truly to live and to grow in holiness. It is a veritable conversion : it makes possible what before was inconceivable ; it brings the soul directly under the powers that by developing restrain it ; that by giving it its true direction gently protect it from the evil influences that would destroy it.

There are those who have not yet entered into this view of life, and who consequently are timid, fearful, always dreading evil which they fear will overmaster them ; there is in their life little of Christian liberty and expansiveness and no joy. A vast part of their nature remains untouched by grace ; there are the germs or virtues in them which have never been developed; they hold back through fear from many a sphere of usefulness; there is a constant introspection and self-analysis; they seem never to be able to get out of themselves; they live in an atmosphere of spiritual self-consciousness; there is no such thing possible for them as self-abandonment in trustful love, but always a restless sense of insecurity; no confidence in God or in the power of His grace; their thought of God is rather as judge than Saviour. All through life they are haunted by a sense of failure and of unfulfilled possibilities. Such persons are indeed strict and hard upon themselves—sometimes too hard. Religion has little in it that can give them joy or peace; they are like people who are morbidly anxious about their physical health, constantly fearing illness and watching their symptoms, but never perceiving that such a condition of things makes health impossible. They are not trying to live; they are only trying not to die. Such people are as

Christians unconsciously living in the spirit of Judaism—a life of restriction and prohibition.

And then there comes a change ; they pass into another atmosphere where love reigns, where positive action takes the place of mere watchfulness and self-restraint ; they launch out into the deep, put forth their powers, and strive to live rather than not to die—to do good rather than not to do evil, to put forth all their strength and energy in the loving service of God and man. They live in that large sphere of positive action and aim that enables them very soon to leave far behind those evil things that they were so long striving to keep from doing. They pass upwards into the life of the Beatitudes, and gain a new revelation of the possibilities of religion, of its wonderful capacity of setting the soul free to live a life of ever-increasing interest and joy.

CONTRITION.

THE virtue which for obvious reasons we should consider first is Contrition. For those who have lost their baptismal innocence can only be saved as penitents. Which of us can think that we have kept our garments in their baptismal purity ? If we have not, then the foundation of our Christian character, upon which all must rest, is penitence. So completely can this virtue stamp itself upon the whole character that we can describe many a person in one word— a 'penitent.' Just as innocence shines out through every virtue in those few choice souls who have preserved it, and gives a special radiance and light to all they do or say, so penitence marks the whole man : it gives its own tone and colour to everything ; it represents to us a definite character in spite of all else that goes to make up the character, and leaves its impress upon every virtue and grace ; the other virtues get a special tone from this, the purity of S. John is different from the purity of S. Augustine : in the one it was never lost ; in the other it was lost, and fought for, and regained ; one had the purity of innocence, the other the purity of penitence.

Penitence, therefore, works as a great force in the soul, moulding and shaping the whole character, the spring of all its movements ever acting upon the will, impelling and restraining it in all things.

And the life of penitence springs from the grace of contrition, that sorrow for sin whose source is in the love of God whom the sinner has offended.

It begins, no doubt, in many less perfect forms. A real penitence may take its rise from the sense of one's own personal loss. 'How many hired servants of my Father have bread enough and to spare, and I perish with hunger.'[1] Such was the beginning of the life of penitence in the Prodigal, but it was only the beginning; it must rise higher than that; such a sense of loss could not brace the will up; for all it has to do and to endure and to forego, it can lead the soul a certain way; it can lead it back to his Father's embrace, and then it passes under the control of a stronger and more enduring power, the love of the Father who has been offended; then it cries 'Against Thee only have I sinned.'

Thus it may be said that there are two conversions: the conversion from sin to self, and the conversion from self to God. In the first stage the thought of God is indeed present, but the

[1] S. Luke xv. 17.

sense of one's own misery and loss is the strongest ; in the second stage the thought of self has almost disappeared ; the soul is glad to suffer, complains of nothing, rejoices if by all it has to endure it can make reparation to the love of God against which it has sinned.

Contrition, then, in a more or less perfect form, is to be found at the very beginning of the spiritual life of all who have ever sinned deeply. It is its first movement, that which causes it to say, ' I will arise.' It is the first thought that breaks in upon the soul as it awakens to the sense of its sin. ' When he came to himself he said, How many hired servants of my Father have bread enough and to spare, and I perish with hunger. I will arise and go to my Father!' The Prodigal awakened to a sense of sin and its misery, and this produced a resolution of the will, ' I will arise and go to my Father '; it was the dawn of the spiritual life amidst all the squalor and degradation that sin had brought in its train. Where the sense of sin is not, the spiritual life cannot exist ; as the life of holiness grows, the spirit of contrition deepens. It seems strange, but it is undoubtedly true, that contrition deepens in proportion as the soul becomes more pure, that is, in proportion as the guilt of sin is removed.

This virtue stands, then, at the entrance of the life of devotion and prayer, waiting to receive the soul and lead it onward in the pathway of holiness, and there is no grace which it does not help to form, over whose development it does not preside, and into which it does not impart something of its own stern yet gentle spirit.

If it is to exist at all, it must reign supreme, and penetrate everywhere. Many a Christian virtue owes its nameless and undefined grace to the fact that its fibre has been woven by the firm yet gentle hands of contrition. It would not have grown, it never could have lived, but for the strong, tender care of that grace which can produce virtues so strangely unlike itself, so apparently opposite to itself. In a soil, barren if it had not been watered by her tears, those virtues were planted, beneath the burning sun of temptation that would have scorched them if she had not sheltered them with her shadow they grew and developed and blossomed, and bore fruit. Who could have ever guessed that the power which unsealed the lips of that shy, reserved person, and enabled him to speak with sympathy and love, was the deep sense of his own sin, and the longing to do something to repair its effects, or that the power which gave strength, determination, perseverance to that will that never could resist temptation, was the very memory of all that it had yielded to in the past, love grieving over its offences, and restoring the power lost by sin !

Yes ; we can little tell the source of the power or the immeasurable strength of the force which sets the long clogged wheels and rusted springs of the spiritual life in motion, and produces such a wonderful result ; and least of all is that soul in whom this grace is working such wonders, conscious of what is taking place within it ; for the strange thing is, that while for the penitent contrition is the mother of all virtues, she is herself the outcome of sin, and while weaving the holiest virtues, she sees how stained her hands are, and seeks to wash them with her tears.

For she can never forget the past ; she is the child of that past, the offspring of the mystical union between the love of God and the memory of sin ; and yet the remembrance of the evil past does not hold her back, nor make her timid, or morbid, or over-introspective ; her very strength consists in, and depends upon, the perfectly healthy tone of the mind. She knows the evil of the past, but she only remembers it in the presence of her Saviour who has pardoned her. She cannot think of her sins but as forgiven ; yet the very certainty of the forgiveness makes the pain of recalling them more keen, but robs it of every vestige of morbidness or self-consciousness.

And thus there is nothing that she will not dare. She will strive after the virtues that seem to belong only to those who have been always kept pure. Despair cannot exist where she is, nor timidity. Though in another sense there is none so timid, timid she must be, remembering the past, yet not timid in the sense that she is afraid to face dangers, and to aim at the very highest.

She is the life and centre of all the soul's

strength and progress. When hope begins to get clouded it is because contrition begins to fail. When faith grows dim and love grows cold, it is because contrition has lost her strength, and is dying. Nay; so clear is her own vision of God, so certain is she of her own love, that she can encourage and sustain the soul in times of utmost darkness and deadness. At these times she is up and awake, and all her strength and tenderness is expended in keeping the soul from fainting. She speaks to it again and again with accents of encouragement and inspiration. 'You have deserved to lose the sense of love and clearness of faith. Why should you expect all to be clear when you remember the years in which you did not try, did not want to believe? Fight on bravely now, and the light and peace will come again.'

It is at such moments that contrition shows her unfailing strength, or at times that are even worse, when old temptations come back with redoubled force, when the power of habit reasserts itself, when all the succours of grace seem to be withdrawn, and the soul is left face to face with the multitude of her enemies, only conscious that the will has no strength to resist ; then it is that contrition comes to the rescue, and her power is felt as never before. Her power, and yet she herself seems so weak, for the inspiration of love seems to have died out of her too ; yet still she is there in the thick of the fight, standing by the will, urging it on with arguments, appealing to it, strengthening it ; and when every fortress of the soul seems won, contrition holds the will and gains the victory.

Thus contrition is indeed the moulding and controlling force that forms, restores, and preserves the penitent. Its transforming power is so great that it can fit the greatest sinner for the company of the saints. The Magdalene was

not out of place by the side of the spotless
mother. Penitence can give to the soul what it
would seem as if it could only gain by innocence.
It verily can 'raise up the poor out of the dust,
and lift up the beggar from the dunghill to set
him among princes, and to make him inherit
the throne of glory.'[1]

Let us proceed to consider some of the characteristics of contrition by which we may test
ourselves whether we are gaining any of its spirit.

1. Contrition is patient : it is ready to endure
all that comes upon it, whether justly or un-
justly ; it knows what it deserves, and it knows
that if others knew it as it truly is it could be
treated with no consideration or kindness. It
recognises that it has no rights ; that the chief
reason that it is permitted to live is in order
that reparation may, in some degree, be done
for the past. It bears about within itself an

[1] 1 Sam. ii. 8.

awakened conscience which speaks as the repre-
sentative of the justice of the all-holy God, and
the voice of conscience is ever passing sentence
upon it, and the soul, in the spirit of penitence,
is ever more and more ready to welcome everything as acting toward it for the satisfaction of
an offended God ; nay, it longs to find new
offerings to make, for it can never lose sight of
God's love, and it knows that whatever it may
have to suffer is not a mere penalty sent in
anger, but a loving chastisement to restore and
perfect it. And it accepts above all things the
consequences of past sin without a murmur,
the constant presence of temptation, the sense
of weakness and of loss, the deadness of heart,
the poverty of prayer, the very fear of self-
deception, the agony of doubt which at times
darkens all the path, filling it with uncertainty,
whether its penitence is real or whether, after all,
it is not a specious form of self-interest. Even

this it learns to bear, and by bearing to overcome. Sometimes when tempted to doubt
whether there can be pardon for one who has
sinned so deeply it triumphs by an all-enduring
act of self-surrender saying, ' Well, if I am to
go to hell even that I will bear as my desert.
For hell itself cannot make me cease to grieve
for having offended God,' and thus it conquers
even the fear of hell. And it endures patiently
the loss of all that it has forfeited, even its best
gifts. As God has withdrawn them it puts away
the desire for them, and it knows if they are to
be regained it must be by a growing transforma-
tion of itself. It longs not so much to receive
anything as to regain the love of God which it
has forfeited. And what if the power of old
sin asserts itself and it yields again and falls?
Even then it does not lose patience or despair,
but with a deeper sense of need strives to cling
more closely to God. Despair or deep dis-

couragement after a fall is the result of depend-
ence upon self, a subtle form of pride. True
contrition knows that any moment in which the
soul lets go of God it plunges into the depths of
its own weakness, and therefore if it fail it takes
the warning saying, ' Why art thou cast down
O, my soul ? and why art thou disquieted within
me ? Hope in God : for I shall yet praise Him,
who is the health of my countenance, and my
God.[1] '

2. Contrition is strong. It shows its strength
by what it puts away rather than by what it does.
It puts away those things with which it has for-
merly sinned. If by necessity it has them as
part of its life, it puts them away from the heart.
That which has been an occasion of sin must be
a memorial of sorrow. We may be violent in
active antagonism to sin, while we are continually
recurring to objects which have been the causes

[1] Psalm xliii. 5.

of sin ; but contrition puts them away, and that at whatever cost. We may hate sin very much, and yet feel that we must have certain things, indulgences, friendships, which have been the cause of sin in the past. So far we are lacking in contrition. We have the element of hate, but not of love. The love of God strengthens the soul to put away from itself what has caused it to offend God. How can it love God and enjoy what has been the means of separating it from Him ? No ; it has but one great longing to return to God : ‘ I will arise, and go to my Father ’ —one great fear—sin. And ‘ love is stronger than death.’ And in the strength of that love, tempered with the fear of sin, it can give up anything ; no gain, no result, could make it tolerate the occasion of sin. What strength it needs to break with things that have become almost a part of our life from long habit ; what strength to break with companionships that are so sweet, albeit so dangerous! The penitent soul needs indeed to be strong, and strength is always calm. It is not merely in moments of spiritual excitement that it deals sternly with itself, relapsing into ease and self-indulgence, when the clearness of spiritual perception has passed, and dulness and chill have settled down on heart and mind. No, it is as calmly firm in the darkest as in the brightest times. When all the lower nature cries out for rest and ease, and God has withdrawn every token of His presence and love, the will remains firm in the practise of self-denial. And again, when God grants to it moments of joy, when it has no doubt, no fear, when the assurance of its acceptance and of God's love comes upon it with an overwhelming rush of emotion, it does not permit itself to be carried away; in the midst of all that inner joy there is the firm grasp upon itself and things around it, and it quietly perseveres in its penitential exercise. How strong

D

it is. How faithful. How unbending towards the offender—the chief of sinners.

3. And once more, contrition is tender. It has no harshness. It springs from the love of God. It does not come before the mind as a duty, it springs out of the heart by the necessity of its own inspiration. It is the longing of a soul burdened with the sense of defilement to be conformed to the holiness of Him whom it loves. It springs from the love of God, not from the hatred of sin ; we cannot rise to love by hatred, but we must pass on from the love of God to the hatred of what He hates. The inspiration of contrition is love, not hate ; there is no taint of bitterness or irritation towards self. Thus, stern and unbending in its self-discipline, it is nevertheless always tender. It bears deeply marked upon itself both the strength and the tenderness of love. It has a 'heart of fire towards God, a heart of flesh towards man, a

heart of steel towards self.' There is an asceticism that is harsh and stern and cruel, but it is not the asceticism of the Christian penitent. There is none so tender towards others, so sensitive for their wellbeing, so slow to condemn or to see others' faults. It seems to it as if all the world needs kindness and care except itself. Contrition closes the eyes towards other sins and opens them upon its own, sees itself as the one culprit in the midst of a world that throbs with the love of God.

Patience, strength, tenderness! A spirit that can endow the selfish, sensual, worldly, easy-going nature with such graces must indeed be mighty. It is. It is as strong as the justice, as gentle as the love, as patient as the mercy of God.

MORTIFICATION.

LET us consider next the spirit of mortification, which is at once the necessary outcome and the guardian of contrition, for, in proportion as the spirit of mortification fails, contrition is certain to die out of the soul, and if there be no true contrition, and the soul longs to gain it, one of the surest ways is by mortification. One whose heart is truly penitent, who lives constantly before God, confessing himself a sinner and deserving His condemnation, will instinctively put away many things from his life that are the tokens of a pleasure-loving nature ; the outer life is bound to take expression from the inner, and if the penitence be deep and strong, it will not be possible but that there should be the outer tokens of it. If there are no such tokens, we must doubt the reality of the penitence.

Yet the practise of mortification is not easy. It not only makes great demands upon the will, but it needs much wisdom and prayer to practise it.

It is strange how often people are to be found who certainly practise mortification and that in no small degree, who live really ascetic lives, allowing themselves very little in the way of enjoyment or indulgence, and yet who most certainly are not mortified in the proper sense of the word, but, on the contrary, are full of self-will and a certain kind of self-indulgence.

It is necessary, therefore, that in the practise of mortification we should be quite clear what our aim ought to be, and where the danger of self-deception lies, for there is no part of our nature in which self-deception acts with greater subtlety and disaster than in the higher aims of

the spiritual life. It would seem almost inconceivable that a person should deny himself in
many things that he liked ; that he should lead
a really austere life, and yet that it could be
possible that all this should be a subtle form of
self-indulgence, yet it undoubtedly is true. For
it is unquestionably true that there may be a
very wide difference between the Christian spirit
of mortification and asceticism regarded as mere
austerity.

There is a strange pleasure to certain temperaments in practising self-torture themselves :
it is an end in itself, it reaches out towards nothing, grasps nothing higher ; it is the morbid
pleasure of inflicting pain upon oneself; it
appears to be a greater pleasure to some natures
to forego what they like than to take it. This
is one of those mysteries of nature which it
is impossible to understand ; but such a spirit
of mortification has nothing to do with Chris-

tianity: it is to be found all over the world, and it is often the source of the most dangerous form of pride.

But Christian mortification is wholly different in its motive and its aim. To most people, the motive whence it springs must be penitence; it is the putting away of things that in themselves are lawful because of past sin; the remembrance of past self-indulgence makes the soul long to forego more and more in the spirit of reparation; it ever stands in this fair world, before God, self-condemned, and feeling that it has not the same rights that others have to the free use and enjoyment of all that is good in the world. There is nothing that it has not abused, it has allowed the creature to crowd out the thought of and the love of the Creator; therefore, in the spirit of self-condemnation, it puts away one thing after another.

In such acts of self-denial there is no harsh-

ness, no hard condemnation of the things that
are put aside ; on the contrary, the penitent soul
realises that the evil lies not in these things but
in itself. All these things are good ; they are
God's creatures, but they have been abused, and
they are put aside with an ever-deepening feeling of its own unworthiness. It feels keenly how
sin has marred the order of God's creation, has
put man in a false relation to all these things ;
it has given them a hold upon him, he has
sunk under their influence, they have enslaved
him ; instead of raising him to God, he has
allowed them to drag him down and to blind
him, so that he cannot see God.

Consequently there is no condemnation of
those things which he willingly foregoes ; indeed,
the mind becomes purified by penitence, so as to
see deeper into their meaning and their beauty,
and to appreciate their real value more. The
penitent soul does not, in stripping itself of all

that is fairest in the world, look upon the world with the jaundiced eye of Puritanism, but with a tender love, weeping over his own sin and weakness, which makes him incapable of using what, had he been more true, he might have used, and in using risen through them to God. Nor does he condemn others who do not put away things which he does ; no, he feels that his own position is an exceptional one : he is a penitent, one who has abused God's good gifts and therefore does not deserve nor dare to have them. But with others it is different; others, he feels, are not like him, and while stripping himself more and more of all but the barest necessity, he will with the utmost tenderness try to protect others from the deprivations he practises himself.

And thus penitence as the motive for mortification protects him who practises it from hardness and pride on the one hand, and, on

the other, from a false condemnation of those
things which he surrenders as if they were evil
in themselves. As he loosens himself from the
dominion of the creatures which had enslaved
and blinded him, he understands and appre-
ciates as he never did before their value and
their beauty, and he perceives how it is possible
for man to rise through them to God. It is
impossible therefore to condemn them as evil;
he has traced evil to its true source, and has
found that it lies in his own heart and will.

Thus in the most mortified and ascetic life,
amidst the barest surroundings, stripped of all
save the merest necessities, living in the utmost
poverty, like Him of whom it was said : 'Foxes
have holes, and the birds of the air have nests,
but the Son of man hath not where to lay His
head,'[1] amidst circumstances as hard and stern
as these, the Christian displays the most perfect

[1] S. Matt. viii. 20.

tenderness and gentleness of heart, the clearest
sense of the real value of all things, the intensest
appreciation of the beauty of nature and the
profoundest humility. The school of self-
discipline and mortification in which he has
placed himself has done its work, and has
proved that it is based upon a true principle by
the wonderful blending of the most opposite
virtues, gentleness and strength, self-condemnation and the appreciation of others—the
putting away as evil for him what is valued and
esteemed more and more as good in itself. If
there were any trace of bitterness, any faintest
taint of Manichæan condemnation of God's
creatures, any hardness towards those who were
not led to a similar life of mortification, we
might condemn it, as based upon a wrong
principle, but when we see the result we cannot
but feel that a principle producing such results
must be founded on truth.

But the spirit of mortification does not spring from penitence alone; it grows out of the condition of our life here on earth. It is necessary for all who would be true to God and themselves. As man was originally created, God was supreme Master of his heart and will. He saw, he knew his end, to love God above all things and to serve Him. And he found himself in a world beautiful and attractive, in which every created thing spoke to him of God and pointed him upwards. His nature had many needs, and he found around him all that would supply these needs provided by the loving hand of God, and in satisfying the wants of nature he was drawn more closely to God. His eye was, as it were, illuminated, so that it could pierce through all and see God in all. He took what his nature needed with unerring instinct and without fear or danger of indulgence; all was in order within him and without, and God was over all and in all.

But with the fall all this was changed. Man had chosen the creature before the Creator, and the creatures enslaved and blinded him. He no longer found that created things lifted him up to God, but that they became an end in themselves. By the order of his creation he needed the creatures ; he could not live without them, for they were meant to lead him constantly to God. But now they came between him and God and held him down. As he used them he found himself more and more blinded and enslaved by them. His whole relationship to them was overthrown, the balance was lost ; he could no longer see clearly the meaning and purpose of things nor rise through them to God : his will got entangled and his senses ensnared.

The instinct that guided him was gone. He was moving about amidst things that but now lifted his whole being Godward, into the mystery of whose existence he saw as into a crystal stream. And now he moves amongst them as one fascinated and bewildered. He found himself guided in the choice or rejection of things by their appearances and their power of giving pleasure, not by the only true principle, their effects in leading him to or holding him back from God. And thus he judged things by their immediate effects upon himself, and finding in them the power of satisfying many wants of his nature, he took all that his unbalanced nature desired, and did not perceive that created things were gaining a faster and tighter grip upon him, till they filled the whole horizon of his soul and shut out God. And as time went on, every step onward created new wants which Nature supplied from her exhaustless treasury, and the satisfaction of all these wants bound man more fast to earth and to the creatures.

How quickly they ensnare, how easily they blind, how rapidly our needs increase we all know but too well. The man of many needs crowds round his life such vast supplies of earthly and material things that the heart becomes deadened and ceases even to desire spiritual things. How *can* it rise, bound down on every side? Yet all these things are in themselves good; they are indeed meant to be channels of approach to God—revelations of God—but the channels have become clogged, the creatures have become opaque, and at last they form a barrier between the soul and God.

Therefore we have to keep ourselves loose from the creatures. We have to learn to use them as they were meant to be used, as means to an end, and the end is God. We have to use each thing as it comes, to use it or abstain from its use in so far as it leads us to God. If anything helps us Godward, it should be used so far as, neither more nor less than, it leads to God. They are means to an end, and such is the nature of those things which are means or instruments, that we should consider, in regard to them, if they are, and to what extent they are, useful as instruments for the end for which we propose to use them. We have a difficult task before us. We are obliged to use many things which have in them a most remarkable and strange power of working their way into our lives and enslaving us, and we have to learn so to use them as to keep free from their dominion and to rise through them to God.

To do this we need to hold ourselves well in hand, conquering those things which try to conquer us—not allowing ourselves to go to the verge of self-indulgence, but keeping ourselves more and more free from the dominion of those things which were created to be our servants, not our masters. We must learn to gauge our progress, not by the multiplying of our needs but by minimising them. He who could feed the multitude in the wilderness and calm the storm upon the lake said of Himself, ' The foxes have holes, and the birds of the air have nests; but the Son of man hath not where to lay His head.'[1] He who could rule the creatures would not permit them to rule Him. He deliberately set them aside and lived in poverty. What a perversion of ideas it is that we should look upon those who accumulate round themselves riches and all kinds of luxuries, and consequently multiply their needs, as being great. They are not, after all, the masters but the servants of the creatures that rule them. Our Lord's estimate of greatness and true

[1] S. Matt. viii. 20.

happiness was different : ' Blessed are the poor in spirit, for theirs is the kingdom of heaven.' [1]

And all this, standing in the right attitude towards the creatures, needs the constant practise of mortification, the holding heart and will free for God. It is not easy, as we find anything getting too strong a hold upon us, to draw back and keep it in check. Food, sleep, pleasure, and a thousand other things, as we touch them they enchant us and call upon us to give in to their enjoyment as much as we desire. The effort to keep all these things in their place involves a mortified life. To stop short of indulgence, to drive away something that we are afraid is beginning to enslave us till we have taught it its proper place and admit it again later into our life as a useful servant ; to stand amidst the vast multitude of God's creatures with which the earth teems—persons, places, things,

[1] S. Matt. v. 30.

sorrows, joys, pleasure and pains—a free man, enslaved by none but using all fearlessly, neither held back by fear nor attracted by mere pleasure, but using and accepting or rejecting each as it comes, in so far as it leads the soul Godward—this is indeed liberty ; but such liberty can only be purchased by mortification.

And such liberty cannot be gained by the mere action of a determined will. No; the will needs a lever to raise the nature out of the bondage to the creatures. And where shall such a lever be found? The power strongest to move the will is love. And there is but one love that can counteract the attraction of the creatures. The love of Him who being God took into Himself a created nature—the sum and consummation of all the creatures—we turn to Him, we cling to His human nature. He is the way out of the labyrinth in which we are entangled to the Father. As our love to the man Christ

Jesus grows more and more within us, we feel an attraction that lifts us from the earth and gives the soul once more its balance. We submit ourselves to the slavery of His love, whom to serve is to reign. ' If the Son shall make you free, ye shall be free indeed.' [1]

[1] S. John viii. 36.

IV

THE CHRISTIAN MOTIVE.

THERE is nothing more sad to see than an aimless life. Such a life does not necessarily mean that the person who lives it never has an aim, but that the aim is constantly being changed. Many a day may be lived very intensely : sometimes an object of interest may fill and absorb every thought for several days. Indeed it is surprising the amount of force and enthusiasm that is expended upon some passing interest altogether out of proportion to its value. Yet a life with all these changing interests and excitements may, after all, be an utterly aimless life ; its characteristic is, that it is taken up with passing things, not with anything that is permanent.

The chief bond that binds such a life together is its most marked characteristic—changeableness, instability, uncertainty.

For it is the end—the aim—that interprets the life ; we judge people not so much by their attainments as by the tendency, the bent of their life. One may use great and excellent gifts for some unworthy purpose, and even though the purpose may never be attained, we know that it has demoralised the character. We judge one another not so much by what we are as by what we are becoming, trying to be. A person who aims at some noble end in life is noble ; the difference between the commonplace life and that which is above the commonplace lies mainly in the region of motive. Before you can understand why one man, with all his failures and blunders, is so different from another, who is in many things more successful, you must understand what it is that inspires his life. The

person whose life from first to last is inspired
by the noblest aim, however constantly it may
fail, however devoid it may be of the brilliancy
of natural gifts, lives the most noble of lives.

For all the world's coarse thumb and finger could not plumb,
So passed in making up the main amount ;
All instincts insecure, all purposes unsure,
Which count not as the work, but swell the man's account.
Thoughts that could not be packed into a single act,
Fancies that broke through language and escaped.
All that I could not be, all men ignored in me,
This I was worth to God.

What, then, ought to be the aim that inspires
the whole character of one who would live the
best and noblest life on earth ?   Many things
at once occur to us that would appeal to ambition and call for applause ; some necessitating
one great gift, some another ; but the greatest
and most perfect life does not necessarily re-
quire great gifts—it lies open to all : it has, not
rarely, been lived by those who have been below
the average so far as natural endowments are

concerned. It is, indeed, a wonderful homage to the power of a great motive to stamp itself upon and develop character, that there are not a few whose names are known in history only on this account, who otherwise would have been lost in the crowd of the commonplace ; but they were lifted up and made great by the motive that formed and governed their lives.

And what motive, then, lies open to all, can equally be followed by all, and makes all great who follow it ? It seems a very simple one, yet it involves much ; it is to fulfil as perfectly as possible the purpose for which one was created by God and placed here upon earth. 'As God hath distributed to every man, as the Lord hath called everyone, so let him walk.'[1] No one can do better with his life than that, no one can put it to a better use. Any life must be perfect in proportion as it does what it was made to

[1] 1 Cor. vii. 17.

do. There are many lives that are brilliant failures ; they strive after many things which they were never intended to do, and fail in that one thing. In proportion as this purpose is considered and aimed after the life is a success. It seems strange that a reasonable being should never ask himself why he was put upon earth, or that it should not occur to him that the reason must be found in the will of his Creator.

I employ a man to do a certain piece of work for me at a certain price. He comes to me at the end of the day and says, 'I have been very busy all day ; I have spent all my time in doing some work of my own that I was anxious to finish.' I answer, ' But you have not done the work that I employed you to do ; you have been full of your own plans, not mine ; therefore, I shall not pay you.' At the end of the day of our earthly life we have to answer to our Maker whether we have been employed about our own work or about His, whether we have even made an effort to find out what He would have us do.

A life which is inspired by such a motive is sure to be a success, for of this we may be absolutely certain, that each of us *can* fulfil in our life that for which we were created. We cannot be sure that we have the gifts needed for any other purpose ; there is at least a risk about it, but in this there is no risk. For God, in creating us, equipped us for the work for which He created us. We have every gift of nature and of grace, of mind and body, which is needed for this work. These gifts can no doubt be used for other ends, and the more brilliant they are the more diverse the uses to which they can be put. Many, not caring to find out what they were given for, may alto- gether abuse them, or use them for purposes that can never develop them to their full capacity, and consequently the character of the person who possesses them will suffer, and the life will fall short of real success. Often the source of discontent, and restlessness, and lack of peace in a life, which from its power and influence and many gifts is the envy of others, is the half consciousness that the aim is not right, that the powers are not being used for the purpose for which they were given.

It will be an inspiring thought then to keep before us : I have all the powers necessary for a true success in life ; no one is so fitted to do the special work I have to do, to fill the special place which I have to fill as I am myself. God wished a certain work to be done ; He is almighty and all wise, He saw exactly the person best fitted to do it. He might have created one endowed with every conceivable gift, but He created me ; He knew what He was about—it was no accident, I did not come here by chance, but as the result of an intelligent Will. We may try after something that is more to our taste or more showy, or that calls for less exertion and discipline, and so may fail : or we may live in total forgetfulness that we were put here on earth for any purpose at all, or we may waste our life and gifts in fretful discontent with the lot that we are powerless to escape from ; but if we take as the key to life the Will of God, and strive to realise His purpose in our creation, and then to fulfil it, we *must* succeed ; and that success will crown the character with a beauty, an attractiveness, a harmony, and an inward peace which will leave the soul without a doubt that the end is right.

Then, too, God has withheld from us what would not be serviceable to this end ; it is in His goodness that He has not overweighted the soul with what would be useless, or with what might dissipate its strength or obstruct its path.

There are many gifts that we may envy in others, yet if we had them they would only be a hindrance ; if they were necessary for us, God would have given them. We do not stud the handle of a hammer with precious stones ; if we did, we should be afraid to use it for its ordinary work ; and God has not so encrusted out nature with gifts and talents as to blind us to its real purpose. By this means life is made more simple ; many doors are closed at the outset : we feel, or we ought to feel, shut out from various positions and spheres of work or influence that pride or ambition might call us into. Indeed, we know well how difficult it is often to accept our limitations ; and how many people spend their lives in trying to push their way through doors that are very clearly closed against them, but they will not believe it.

Thus each of us has all that is necessary for fulfilling God's purpose in life, and what we have not we need not regret or envy in others. God did not withhold anything in a grudging spirit, but only because it would be in our way.

And the work of life which God calls us to do has one great end—the development and perfecting of our character. It has, no doubt, its own intrinsic value; it would be a most uninspiring view of the work of life to suppose that in itself it was worthless, like some piece of work given a child, only to teach her how to use her needle. We cannot estimate the value of what is done upon earth, we cannot see its issues; but that it has an intrinsic value we cannot doubt. Yet the great end for which *we* have been chosen to do it is for our own development and perfection. We may no doubt do the very work God has put us on earth to do in a way that injures ourselves; but if this be so, we may also feel assured that the work of God must suffer also; if the machine gets out of order, it cannot do its work perfectly.

It is by the work of life, and in the place chosen by God, that the character is to be formed and perfected, and it is by the character deepening in perfection that the work is to be most perfectly done. There is the work and there is the man—they were made for one another—no one can do the work so well as he, and no other work can do so much for that man. Such a thought will give interest and value to all we have to do, and raise the smallest and most insignificant duties out of the commonplace. Those uninteresting surroundings, and dull people, and that round of duties, they are the tools with which God carves and chisels out of our nature the likeness of Christ ; to neglect anything, to do anything in a careless and perfunctory way, will not only spoil the work but will injure the worker.

This, then, must be a fundamental and ruling principle in life, the principle of Vocation —of a purpose which we are called to fulfil ;

everything will go wrong if the aim is not right. If the aim be true, it will give force and direct-ness to the whole character, and every power of nature and grace will be developed in its perfect proportion.

The idea of Vocation must not be limited to one or two of the more clearly marked calls of God, such as the call to the priesthood or the religious life ; we read in the Gospels of one who thought he had a call to such a special following of our Lord as the Apostles had, and our Lord forbade him, and said to him, 'Go home to thy friends, and tell them how great things the Lord hath done for thee.'[1] He would have mistaken his Vocation if he had given up everything to follow Christ ; his Vocation, there-fore, was as distinctly to the home life as was St. Peter's to the apostolic life. It is important that we should remember this : Vocation is the call of God to whatever form of life He may

[1] S. Mark v. 19.

please to call one. The *realising* of one's position in life *as a Vocation* is like a conversion, it
is the opening of the eyes to see the purpose
and Will of God behind and through the
ordinary events of life. The parable of the
labourers in the vineyard shows us the mono-
tonous and commonplace life of a day labourer
transformed by the hearing of the call, 'Go,
work in my vineyard.' [1]

In the manifold works and obligations of
life, all that keeps the world going, the fundamental difference lies in this, that multitudes
who fulfil those duties do so because they are
obliged ; some few do them in obedience to the
Will of God, and this makes all the difference
in the character of those who work. Therefore,
while some Vocations are no doubt more clearly
marked than others, everyone, no matter how
humble his position, has his place and work

[1] S. Matt. xx. 4.

F

assigned by God, and consequently has in the true sense of the word a Vocation, the realising and fulfilling of which is the condition of perfection.

We must consider further that all God's action towards us will be directed to perfect us through our Vocation, ' This is the Will of God, even your sanctification ;'[1] it is true, He does care for our happiness and temporal welfare. Everything that affects us is of interest to Him, but all is subservient to our true happiness and the real success of life. If health is necessary that we should reach this end, we may be assured that we shall have health ; if health would hinder us, it shall be taken from us ; if success is good for us, He will allow us to succeed, but if it would stand in our way, if we would rest in it, or it would elate us and make us worldly, we shall not have success. And so with everything : all is in His hands, and all is ordered with a view

[1] 1 Thess. iv. 3.

to this one end—the fulfilment of the purpose for which He placed us here. And God cannot be won round to forego this. No prayers will move Him. He would be unfaithful to us and to His promises if He failed to fulfil His part. The opportunities, the temptations, the troubles, the blessings will come, the ordering of the outward circumstances of our life ; all this we may be sure of, whether we correspond or not. This mighty Will goes on ordering all as it should if we were faithful.

There is something at once alarming and bracing in this thought : it is alarming, indeed, if we do not care to correspond, to think that the strong currents of God's Will, working towards an end from which we have turned away, still keep beating around us, beating upon us, filling the spaces of our life with movements that all tend in the opposite direction to our own, and that must eventually crush us if we do not turn and yield. And yet bracing too : is it not a bracing and inspiring thought to think that there is the Will of Him who orders all things working towards one end —the end towards which we have turned our life—and that it is always on the side of our best selves, always waging unceasing war against any onesided or partial view of life ; that if we get lax or weak He will not be so unkind as to yield to us ; that if we swerve for an instant to one side or the other, it, as it were, strikes us and forces us back again. What a strength to think that we have no plan, no purpose in life but His whose Will orders all things.

We have thus but to look out upon the circumstances of our life at any moment to see the operation of this Will on our behalf. 'All things work together for good,' if only our will is directed towards the same end as His. A few suggestions may be helpful with a view to training the will to correspond with God's purpose.

1. Try to see the Will of God in little things. 'The very hairs of your head are all numbered,'[1] 'Not a sparrow shall fall on the ground'[2] without His will. Nothing happens in our daily life without His permitting it, even what happens through the sin of others. God does not will sin, but He does permit that, sin being committed, we should be tried by it. It needs the constant exercise of faith and watchfulness to see the Will of God constantly operating towards us.

2. Keep the will free when anything naturally pleasing offers itself, some opportunity of enjoyment, some plan that you would naturally like ; wait before you decide, and look to God, consult His Will before you choose—that pause

[1] S. Luke xii. 7.   [2] S. Matt. x. 29.

and prayer may make all the difference in the result of your choice.

3. So, too, in times of uncertainty, make constant acts of self-oblation, keep your will free till you know the Will of God. Many a time such periods of uncertainty are permitted as times of preparation ; during that time of waiting the will learns to accept what it perhaps could not have accepted at once.

4. Do not throw too much intensity into the legitimate choices of the will in ordinary things that give enjoyment. Hold much of the power of the will in reserve ; don't spend and exhaust its powers in things which are not worth it. With certain temperaments the tendency is to choose passionately and with all the intensity of one's nature the passing pleasures or superficial things of life as well as the deeper and more important, and consequently there is a lack of proper detachment

and readiness to forego what one may have to give up. Keep yourself in hand and reserve the whole power of the will's choice for those things that are worth it.

5. Remember there is a vast difference between willing and wishing ; you can't help what you wish at any given moment, but your will is in your own power. Your wishes are the inclinations of your nature, as you find them now, from whatever cause, temperament, taste, or perhaps past sin. It can't be helped *now*, but often the greatest triumphs of grace consist in the will choosing in direct opposition to what nature wishes. You can't help wishing not to say your prayers, or not to fast, or not to get up in the morning, but you can *will* and determine to act in opposition to these wishes and so to grow in strength and grace. Therefore don't be anxious because many times you don't *wish* to do God's Will—*will* to do it, *do* it,

and the triumph and the reward will be all the greater.

And so, in spite of, and through, all the obstacles both within and without that beset the pathway of the soul, it presses on to fulfil the purpose of God.

V.

SELF-OBLATION.

THERE are many things that belong to man's life on earth in his fallen state that will cease with his earthly condition. Much of his life and thought is necessarily taken up with such things. It is a strange contrast that is presented by the seriousness of life as we are taught it in Holy Scripture and the multitude of trifles and superficial things that fill up the days of so many of us, yet no doubt all these things have their value in the discipline of character.

And there are many virtues that can only be developed under the present conditions of life, such as faith, contrition, patience, though these virtues, rooted deeply in our nature, will bear their perfect fruits in eternity. What the effect of an ever-deepening penitence on earth will be when the soul has been cleansed from every consequence of sin and sees God face to face through eternity, we cannot tell ; or what the result of the discipline of a life of faith when faith is lost in vision, we cannot tell ; or what place an enduring patience that has been fought for so bravely here can have in the soul that can never again be thwarted or tried, we do not know ; though we can readily see that one trained in such a school, when he passes upward out of the present condition of things, bears within him a certain tone of character that can develop, under other circumstances, into other types of perfection of which these may be but the seeds and roots, just as there seems but little connection between the lessons and discipline of the schoolroom and the developed powers of some great statesman or artist.

It may perhaps be that all those virtues that especially belong to our condition here on earth will develop into the one perfect and many-sided grace of love—a love that has been tested in every conceivable way, and comes forth from the fires purified and unchangeable.

But there are some ruling principles of the Christian life whose continuity we can see more clearly; there are virtues and practices begun here that are to be continued through eternity. Worship, praise, adoration, the love of and submission to the Will of God—these, and many other such habits, are to be exercised for ever. Here, indeed, they are to be learnt under circumstances that form our probation; there they are to be our joy. But there is an orderly growth and development in these graces; the soul that struggles with itself against all that would lead it away, to cling to and obey the Will of God, will find its eternal joy in living beneath the perfect rule of that Will ; all that is counter to it will have passed away, and it will know that to 'serve Him is to reign.' So again the efforts after worship and praise amidst all the distractions and temptations of life, prompted and supported by faith, will be crowned by the glorious worship of heaven in the full vision of God. Habits are being formed here under the pressure of temptation and difficulty that unfold in perfect form and beauty when the soul that has developed these habits passes into its true home. Those very temptations which made it so difficult to persevere were really the means of developing these powers. The spirit of prayer and worship grew on ; hampered and oppressed by the distractions of life, it fought its way in spite of them and thus gained strength ; then, when all these were removed, it opened out unhindered in its perfect growth.

Now there is one fundamental principle of the spiritual life that has to be learnt and practised here, mostly with suffering, often with the very keenest suffering, sometimes even involving the sacrifice of life itself; and yet suffering, though so closely associated with it that it almost seems a necessary part of it, is indeed only accidental, and one day will altogether cease, while the grace that has been fought for and developed in so much agony will live on for ever, and be the delight of the soul through eternity. I mean the principle of sacrifice and self-oblation.

In the worship described in the vision in the Apocalypse 'the four-and-twenty elders fall down before Him that sat upon the throne and worship Him that liveth for ever and ever, and cast their crowns before the throne.' [1] They lay their crowns, the symbol of their attainments, at the

[1] Rev. iv. 10.

Feet of Him that sitteth upon the throne ; and while these glorified saints are thus offering themselves in delighted homage in heaven amidst surroundings that tell of perfect joy and peace, some poor struggling Christian upon earth has broken away with tears and an aching heart from what he loves most that he may do more thoroughly what he believes to be the Will of God. The principle that moves both is the same --sacrifice and self-oblation—only here the will is being purified and cleansed, loosening itself with pain from the creatures to which it clings inordinately, that in faith, and often with little sensible love, it may give itself to God. There, in that picture in heaven, we see the result ; there is no more need of struggle or effort, the will is free, bound for ever into the Will of God, and it is the joy of the soul for eternity to cast itself and all it possesses at the Feet of its Creator.

Suffering, in our present state, is indeed an integral part of the life of sacrifice, so much so that we scarcely think of sacrifice as apart from suffering; but it is good for us, when we are called upon to make the most painful sacrifice, to remember that there is no necessary connection between the two ideas. Originally there certainly was none ; when Adam stood in Eden, clad in the garment of original righteousness, and cast himself in worship before God, it was his supremest joy to offer himself ; there was no obstacle between him and God to hold him back, no barrier obstructing the will through which it had to force its way. And certainly the hosts of angels knew no life apart from God, and have no will save His ; yet their life of heavenly joy and peace, into which no pain or discord has ever entered, is a life of sacrifice. So far as we know, there is but one spot in creation where there is any association between

suffering and sacrifice, or where there is associated with obeying the Will of God any idea of
difficulty or pain, and that is here on earth.
For here sin has entered and set up barriers
between man and God ; but we look backward
and forward, and we see that originally it was
not so, and hereafter it shall not be so. Such
a condition belongs only to our present state ;
here we must fight our way in spite of all the
obstacles that seek to hold us back from doing
God's Will, knowing that whatever it cost us, it
is our only true life, and that the struggle and
the pain are the conditions of our regaining our
true relationship to Him and for ever rejoicing
in His Will.

We may look up, then, when conscience calls
us to make some great and painful sacrifice and
say, 'The pain only belongs to my present state ;
countless multitudes of my fellow-creatures find
such acts of sacrifice their greatest joy, the pain

will soon cease, for the will will soon know that its completest life is in following the Will of God ; meanwhile every struggle and painful choice for God helps to restore the balance which sin has destroyed, turning the will away from the Creator to the creature.'

It is, then, in following the Will of God, in spite of all difficulties that may arise both from within and from without, in the constant offering of ourselves to God as the creatures of His hand to do and to be what He would have us, in the surrender of one thing after another that comes between us and Him and holds us back—it is in such acts that we unite ourselves with those glorious beings who cast their crowns before the throne, and with those unfallen creatures who have never known what it is to have a wish or thought apart from the Will of God. Amongst those glorified saints there are, indeed, many whose wills were for a long time in revolt against

G

God's Will, and who brought themselves at last into subjection, many to whom the Will of God here on earth meant the sacrifice of everything the heart most loved, many to whom it meant the sacrifice of life itself. But all that is past and over, and its fruits alone remain—the eternal life of oblation and union with God, where one Will rules those countless multitudes and binds them together and to God, where each one of those countless millions lives his own complete and perfect life yet never jars on any other, where each is perfect in itself and all together compose one perfect whole—the Body of Christ. This is the outcome of that life of sacrifice and discipline on earth ; it is for this that the will has to be so constantly broken in, and that God demands of us what costs so much, every act of painful sacrifice helping to cleanse the will of its obstinacy, selfishness, adherence to the creatures, until, brought completely under the control of

God, the soul is ready to take its place in the glorified Body.

Or, to put it in another way, man was created under the law of sacrifice. It is the fundamental law of the creature's life to surrender himself wholly to his Creator's Will. In fulfilling this law he found his own perfection and his own completest happiness. Then came the fall, when man fell from his life of union with God, and chose the creature rather than the Creator, and thus gave the creatures a power over him which they had not originally, and raised up barriers between him and God. But still the law of his life remained ; his truest happiness and his only perfection consisted in living the life of self-oblation. But now all kinds of difficulties beset his path if he would live this life ; much of his time had to be taken up, if he would live, in things that only concerned the present, and seemed to have no relation to God or the future ; the penalty inflicted upon him at his expulsion from Eden, 'in the sweat of thy face shalt thou eat bread,'[1] bound together the preservation of his life with labour. If he would not work he could not eat ; and what connection could there be between such labour and the worship of God? Its tendency was, as we know too well, to drag him down and make him less spiritual. The life of toil does drag down and weary the mind, and it is hard for the labourer to realise as he goes forth day after day to his work and to his labour till the evening, that this nature, which seems to fit itself so aptly to the life of the beast of burden, was made for worship and for God. Yet, however worn out and wearied with toil, however clouded the mind may be with care and too tired to think, the law of man's life still remains unchanged; his only true happiness and perfection is to be found in the life of sacrifice.

[1] Gen. iii. 9.

But not only did this law of labour make it difficult for him to live the life of worship and oblation ; there were other difficulties which beset his path at every step. Opposition coming from others, sometimes inspired by hate, sometimes by the love of those who would hold him back by their tenderness from doing what seemed so hard, often conflicting claims of duty when the rights of others seemed to stand in the way of fulfilling what appeared to be the Will of God, and those countless trials which clip the wings that would soar upward and drag the soul down to earth, the irritations and sorenesses that spring from the thoughtlessness of others, the lack of sympathy that makes life so chill, the miserable mistakes by which the most ill-assorted lives are bound together, bringing in their train a multitude of temptations which rob the soul of any power to rise to God, the irresponsiveness of those we would help, and the countless worries and vexations which cloud the atmosphere and drive the soul steadily downward to earth. Certainly many who recognise the law of self-oblation have found it so difficult to fulfil that they have given it up as hopeless.

And then our Lord came, the second Adam, into a world that was disordered by the sin of the first Adam, to show us how to live on earth amidst all these altered conditions true to the primary law of the creature's life. He did not exempt Himself from any of the conditions under which man has to live; He came to show us how it was possible to live amidst all these difficulties the perfect life of sacrifice.

He came down from the midst of the perfect worship of heaven, assumed our nature and lived in it from His birth to His death, in absolute obedience to the great vow of the incarnation, ' Lo, I come to do Thy Will, O my God.' Such was the motto of His life, and He carried it out

perfectly and without swerving, though every
obstacle that man or devil could devise was
thrown in His way. But those very efforts to
hinder Him were made the means by which the
Will of God was worked out. There was, indeed,
but one place where any real obstacle could be
raised, and that was in the will of Him who
came to offer Himself; unless that failed, nothing
else could really hinder Him.

We watch Him, then, entering into the life
we know so well, and passing through those
troubles and temptations which have held so
many down; and we see Him press on, though
obstacle after obstacle was thrown across His
path, but still He never swerves. Sometimes
He has to wait, sometimes to hold back, sometimes to retire, but never for a moment does
He swerve, and rarely if ever does God inter-
vene in the natural order of events to help Him.
No; He must live as we live, under the same

conditions, not a life surrounded or protected by miracles. Men are free : they may listen to or scorn Him, they may try to make Him a king or kill Him ; God leaves the world and leaves His Son, as He leaves us, to fight His way through it, and to answer by His life, not merely by His words, how in such a world man can live true to the law of the creature's life.

At times the difficulties were so great that it seemed as if it would prove impossible to carry out His purpose. Misunderstanding, misrepresentation, unfaithful friends, treachery, deliberate injustice, envy, organised opposition, the slowness of perception of His own most faithful followers, the narrow prejudice of His hearers. On all sides difficulties sprang up, apparently making it impossible for Him to carry out the work He came on earth to do, till finally He was arrested and brought to trial and condemned to death. But meanwhile, within His most holy

Soul, His human Will was ever pressing through all these difficulties upwards towards God. His Will pierced through these things that were meant to hinder Him, and they all formed so many elements in His life of sacrifice. Can anything hinder Him ? No ; for the very obstacles are transformed. They were meant by Satan to block the pathway of the will Godward ; but that strong loving Will forced its way through them and rose, and the effort and struggle enhanced the value of the offering.

See Him at last as He hangs upon the Cross —*the* one great sacrifice of the world, that sacrifice which we constantly plead upon our altars, the central act of our worship. This it was that was forefigured in the gorgeous ritual of the Temple ; it is upon this that we alone rest our hopes, through it alone that we can ever approach God or offer an acceptable prayer. Yet did it look like a great act of worship ? No ;

it looked to all appearances but a terrible scene of cruelty and crime. And so it was; everything that the eye could see or the ear could hear was low, degraded. Was it amidst such scenes, such sounds, that God could be worshipped? It seems a degradation that any noble life should be exposed to such scenes of shame. Yet even there, amidst that vile base mob, the offscourings of the slums of Jerusalem, amidst jeers and blasphemies, the most sublime act of worship and sacrifice ascended before God that had ever been offered on this earth. Nay, more, those very things that crowd around the cross of shame, the words, the deeds, the acts of cruelty, they form, so to speak, the instruments for the offering of this divine liturgy. Rising up through all, transforming, hallowing all, was the pure Will of Him who hung upon the cross, accepting, offering all to God, and using the sins of men and the pain and humiliation which their sins brought upon Him, as elements by which the value of His offering was enhanced.

Yes, by stooping so low, by permitting Himself to be the victim of all that hatred and envy, He shows us that there are no circumstances so low, no trials so humiliating, that they cannot be transformed by the will that rises through them and offers them to God.

This, then, is the lesson of our Lord's Life and Passion. All difficulties, all sufferings, all obstacles that cross our path to hinder us from offering ourselves to God,—all these are to be looked upon as the instruments of our sacrifice : we are to use them, to rise through them. The will forcing its way through such opposition makes the sacrifice more costly.

In the sacrifice of our Lord there were things both great and small—the teasing thorns and the cruel nails, the jarring voices of the ignorant mob, and the cold-blooded villany of Caiaphas. So it is with us, things great and small take their part in consummating our sacrifice : the irritations arising from those we live with who do not understand us or who are not congenial, the cutting word that wounds our pride, the weariness and monotony of life's routine, the drag of our earthly nature that will not rise, the uninteresting, unexciting, commonplace duties, ill health—all these things and a thousand more that torment us day by day and seem sometimes to take all power of resistance from us ; and the greater trials—strong temptations, bitter disappointments, failures, sorrow, bodily pain, loss of friends—all these tend to keep the will down or to rouse it to revolt ; but as we struggle through them, making acts of oblation and acceptance, clinging, while the lower nature cries out in pain, still clinging to God and offering them up, then we are following the lesson of our Lord's life, using life's difficulties as the instruments of our sacrifice. Every time we offer up the Holy Sacrifice we offer it with deeper meaning, and bring its lessons into our daily life, we learn to live the life of sacrifice. It was the genius of sanctity which transformed that which had been the symbol of shame into the symbol of all that is noblest, holiest, highest, and we in our measure and degree as we draw closer to Him can transform the lowest, poorest, most humbling of our troubles by the way we bear it, seeing in every trial a part of our cross, an instrument of our Passion, and looking on to that eternal life beyond, where countless myriads live the life of perfect oblation, and cast their crowns before the throne with the joy and peace that has been gained through the cross and sufferings of earth.

VI.

PRAYER.

THE perfect life consists in the perfect correspondence to the Will of God. He who came
to teach us how to live said, 'I came down from
heaven, not to do Mine own will, but the Will
of Him that sent Me'; [1] 'My meat is to do the
Will of Him that sent Me, and to finish His
work;' [2] and St. Paul says of Him, 'Even Christ
pleased not Himself.' [3] In the hour of His
Agony His Prayer was, 'If it be possible, let
this cup pass from Me; nevertheless, not as I
will, but as Thou wilt.' [4] He would not antici-
pate by a moment the appointed work of His

[1] S. John ii. 38. [2] S. John iv. 34.
[3] Rom. xv. 3. [4] S. Matt. xxvi. 39.

life. 'Mine hour is not yet come,'[1] He said
again and again ; but when the hour had come
for work or suffering, He never failed. From
first to last His life was the perfect correspondence with His Father's Will ; His first word was,
'Wist ye not that I must be about my Father's
business?'[2] almost his last, 'It is finished.'[3]
Therefore the more truly we desire to follow
our Lord's example and to attain perfection, the
more deeply must this principle underlie all our
plans and actions ; as we lose sight of this we
are almost certain to get astray, and set up false
standards and unworthy aims.

But such a life involves great self-discipline
and constant sacrifice ; many an ambition has
to be crushed, many an opening for plans that
are much to our taste has to be abandoned.
Any who would live such a life must have their

[1] S. John ii. 4, vii. 31, viii. 20, xiii. 1.
[2] S. Luke ii. 49.   [3] S. John xix. 30.

nature well in hand, and be living in close communion with God. It is an easy thing to say, 'The perfect life is the perfect correspondence with the Will of God,' but it is not easy to carry out in practice, for it is certain to lead us along a rough and difficult path where oftentimes our heart and strength will fail us. If it was so with the Master, we cannot be surprised that it should be the same with the servant.

Two things especially any who would live this life will need. First, the ever-increasing knowledge of God's Will; and, secondly, the grace to correspond with it when it is known. First light and secondly grace—light for the mind, grace for the will. We may know God's Will for us well enough at any given moment, and not have the strength to obey it, or we may at times earnestly desire to follow God's Will and yet not know it. We need both light and grace.

Now, that we may attain these gifts, it is necessary to be living near God. It is impossible for us to turn suddenly from a distracted or careless life and to find ourselves at once illuminated and strengthened. The knowledge of God's Will is often most difficult to attain, even for those living very near Him ; often those who love Him most and are most single-minded are left in doubt as to His purpose for them, and only by constant prayer and self-discipline do they gradually gain the knowledge.

Therefore, if we would not make grievous mistakes, and perhaps make shipwreck of our lives, we must endeavour to keep near God, to learn to know Him better, to understand the tokens of His Will and the method of His dealings with us ; in a word, to get upon terms of loving and reverent friendship with Him.

But this can only be done by prayer. A

II

prayerful life is almost certainly a life of con-
formity to the Will of God ; a prayerless life is
quite certainly a life of self-will, in which imperfections and sins and the spirit of worldliness
cloud the spiritual perception so that it is not
even conscious of how far it is separated from
God.

And yet, while prayer is the condition of
knowing God, there is no practice of the
spiritual life more difficult. To pray well, to
grow in the knowledge of God, we *must* pray ;
and to be able to pray well we have to learn
how to pray, to live through, perhaps, many
years, in which we seem to gain little fruit, and
are often scarcely conscious of any progress.

And, moreover, each has practically to learn
for himself how to pray. We may gain some
encouragement, some little help from others, but
the real secret of prayer we must learn for ourselves. How can anyone teach another the

form of conversation and method of intercourse with a friend? It grows, unfolds, develops of itself; it is intensely personal. We may learn something from the experience of others as to where dangers lie, as to possible self-deception, the need of perseverance through times of darkness and coldness ; but the inmost secret of prayer must be our own. It is the deepest expression of the soul's personal relationship with God. It is, indeed, in one sense like, but in another unlike, the prayer of anyone else. If God has given us any power in prayer, we shall find that it is impossible to communicate the secret of that power to anyone else ; when we try to tell that we fail. We may repeat the prayer that we say, and tell of some of the trials and struggles through which we have passed, but we cannot tell just that thing which gives the power and strength to our prayers, for in fact it is our relationship to God

Himself; it is the expression of all that we mean by our spiritual life.

Yet there are certain dangers that are common to most people, and certain principles upon which growth in the life of prayer must be based.

To many persons it seems, when first they begin in earnest the practise of prayer, that the best guide is their own devotion, that in spiritual matters system and rule crush out all spontaneity and life, and that often even the mere attitude of kneeling chills them and makes them formal. They find that they can pray better at work than on their knees at irregular times of exceptional fervour than at stated times, and that consequently the best rule is to pray when they can pray best. Such persons have a proper dread of formalism, and it seems to them as if system and rule must degenerate into formalism if prayers are to be said at stated times whether there is any fervour of spirit or not. Yet such persons should remember :—

1. That as time goes on those inspirations and times of fervour, unless carefully disciplined, become less frequent and intense, and at last probably die out altogether. They belong to the early years of spiritual youth ; they are given to help the soul in those first arduous struggles with bad habits and sins of the past, but they pass away ; they are not a necessary part of the saintly life ; they are, moreover, full of imperfections, and those who depend upon such states of mind for prayer, will find that as time goes on they pray less, not more.

2. Everything is of value only in so far as it helps to form character. A person whose intercourse with God mainly depends upon the amount of emotional fervour he experiences will not have much strength of will or determination. The life of prayer cannot be built upon any-

thing so unreliable as feelings without being itself unreliable ; it is built rather upon acts of the will. The religious character, therefore, is developed, and more is done for God by system and regularity than by all the fervour and excitement in the world. A great part of the discipline of faith is the holding on to God in darkness ; one, therefore, who goes on regularly with prayer in coldness and deadness as faithfully as in times of the greatest fervour, thanking God when He makes His Presence felt, but not laying too much stress upon it, not gauging his progress by it, but believing that it is the will, fighting its way through darkness and almost the chill of death, which is accepted by God ; such a person's character is altogether a more religious one and a stronger one than the other, and moreover we shall find that he has a far deeper and truer knowledge of God. The effort to get nearer God when He seems far off awakens a longing, and strengthens the will in a way which one can never experience whose prayers depend upon emotion. The religious character that is ruled by impulse is quite a different one from that which is governed by principle. God can reveal Himself in darkness as well as in light ; we are told that ' clouds and darkness are round about Him,'[1] as well as that ' He decketh Himself with light as it were with a garment.'[2] Those, therefore, who will not pray in darkness lose that special revelation which God gives through the darkness, and surely none who have persevered through such times can doubt that God revealed Himself to them then. When the darkness has passed the soul will find what an increased knowledge and love of God it has gained.

3. Then, too, it must be borne in mind that devotion is of two kinds, essential and accidental.

---

[1] Psalm xcvii. 2.   [2] Psalm civ. 2.

The word means 'consecration,' and this consecration is an act of the will—offered, dedicated,
devoted. Essential devotion, then, is devotion
of the will offered to God and independent of
any emotion. He who prays in such a spirit,
offering himself to bear whatever God may
send, is certainly devout whatever he may feel,
though his whole time of prayer be spent in
nothing but a struggle with distraction. God
will not refuse to accept the service of a will
which is devoted to Him. Accidental devotion
arises when there flows in upon the will thus holding on to God the light and joy and peace which
stirs the heart and feelings. This is, after all, but
accidental, it is not of the essence of devotion ;
one may be very devout without it. For the
deepest love is the love that has passed down
into the will and rules there. The love that a
young couple experience in the first days of
their married life is full of passion and feeling ;

but after they have lived together for years and their lives are woven into one another, those passionate feelings of love have mostly given way to a stronger love that rules the will. They probably feel little of what they used to experience, but now each rules and moulds the other's life ; perhaps it is only when there comes the possibility of a separation that either realises how intense their love is.

So it is in prayer. We must not gauge our devotion by what we feel, but rather by what we are ready to endure. Indeed it often happens that God tries the most advanced by letting them experience a coldness and dead-ness in prayer such as ordinary people seldom experience, and none could endure in such times if their love for God were not very deep and strong, ruling and sustaining the will.

Now, in considering the act of prayer itself, we must remember that it is composed of a natural and supernatural element: the act of the person who prays, and the help which God gives. Different classes of minds are in danger of laying undue stress on one or other of these parts as if it comprised the whole, but all true prayer involves both.

Therefore due consideration must be given to both parts. If the best musician in the world were playing on an organ that was out of tune he could not produce good music, and if the Holy Spirit were to breathe over our souls in prayer while the strings were lax from damp or carelessness, He could not produce the music that God loves to hear. Our prayer may fail, therefore, not because God does not help us, but because we have not taken proper care in preparing ourselves; the strings of the mind are out of tune. We shall never get so high as to be able to leave out of consideration our own preparation and discipline. And, on the other hand, if the mind were under perfect control and discipline, we should never be able to pray without the help of God's Holy Spirit. The organ may be in perfect tune, but it needs the hand of the musician to draw out its powers. When we come to our prayers we must place ourselves beneath His influence. 'The Spirit also helpeth our infirmities, for we know not what we should pray for as we ought.'

Let us consider these two elements then, the natural and the supernatural.

1. The natural.

i. The mind must be prepared. So many of our prayers are poor and unworthy because the mind is not properly prepared ; one kneels down with the best disposition, but the mind has got into a morbid condition, and the whole time of prayer is lost in a kind of unhealthy self-examination ; or it is absorbed in some

_____
[1] Rom. viii. 26.

matter that it has allowed to take possession of it, and the time is spent without ever rising up to God. Or again, no sooner does one kneel down than it seems to be the signal for the imagination to break loose and bring before the mind everything one has thought, said, or done, and everyone that one has seen during the day. It is important, therefore, that we should remember that the instrument with which we pray is that with which we do all our other mental work; when we turn it to God we shall find that it has the same defects and the same powers that it has at other times, only that we become more conscious of the defects in times of prayer. No wonder it is difficult to pray if there is no effort made to discipline or concentrate the mind at other times; how can the mind that is left relaxed and unguarded all through the day be recollected in prayer? Prayer is not the only time to struggle against distractions; the more orderly, methodical, disciplined and concentrated our minds are during our daily life, the more we shall be able to direct them to God in prayer.

There is nothing, therefore, that we do during the day which may not prove a help or hindrance in times of prayer. In reading, working, thinking, we are unconsciously training our minds for prayer. If it is the same mind which we use for all our ordinary work which we use in prayer, the same and no other, we shall find the same laxity, the same distractedness, the same slipshod and careless ways, the same habit of losing ourselves in day-dreams at prayer which we experience in all our mental life. It is a good thing, therefore, to remember that prayer is not the time to train the mind, but that in prayer we shall reap the fruits of the carelessness or watchfulness of our ordinary life.

ii. Again, it must be remembered that the

mind is a very delicate instrument, and is very easily put out of order, and that spiritual work does not exempt people from natural laws. We need, therefore, care and common sense just as much in spiritual as in temporal things ; a person may suffer very considerably in his spiritual life from lack of the exercise of a little common sense.

(a) In learning to pray it is, therefore, most important not to overburden oneself at first with too many prayers. Leave plenty of room to grow, be content at first to say such prayers as are suited to a beginner. If you would ever be able to spend a long time in prayer you must begin with short times ; the mind must be seasoned. Do not let prayer hang over you as a burden. It may be an admirable exercise in humility to confess to oneself how short a time one is able to pray ; the mind must grow into the life of prayer, but it will never do this if it is allowed to be overweighted with a burden of prayer beyond its strength.

(b) Again, do not leave your prayers to be said when the mind is too wearied to think. If you are obliged to be up late, say the greater part of your prayers earlier in the evening ; it is a fatal thing to go to one's room at night tired out and burdened with the dread of a considerable time to be spent in prayer, much of which experience has taught will be a mere struggle with sleep. One will never learn to pray by such methods ; the mind needs in prayer the exercise of all its powers, and prayer should be said when the mind is fresh and in full vigour. The times of prayer, therefore, should be arranged so that the natural instrument is at its best, not at its worst, and it should be always borne in mind that God does not give His grace to help us to do what nature can do of itself. You have no right to expect God to help you to say your prayers when you are tired, because you have not taken the trouble to say them in proper time.

(c) There must be, if there is any *life* in prayer, adaptability ; one of the chief conditions of life is the capacity of adapting inward to outward relations.   It is the same with prayer. Prayers in sickness will not be the same as in health if they are the utterances of a living soul, and in times of special trial or temptation the prayers will not be those of one's ordinary life.   The soul, in proportion as prayer becomes a reality, will instinctively adapt its prayers to special circumstances, not lightly indeed changing the form of prayer, but having that liberty of spirit which makes rule not a hindrance but a help, not the destroyer but the developer of life.

2. The supernatural.

But there is also the supernatural element in

prayer. We must, indeed, discipline and train our minds, and fulfil our part ; but prayer is not a mere straining of the mind towards God, we must pray as Members of Christ ; ' He hath made us accepted in the Beloved.' [1] We pray not as those who have nothing to depend upon but their own efforts, but as those whose acceptance is already assured if they have faith to realise their great privileges. We Christians speak, as it were, with the Lips of Christ. We know that in proportion as we believe in and use our great privilege, God cannot reject us. Our own powers may be very limited, the sense of our sins may dismay us, but we draw near with the life of our Lord within us, ' Members of His Body, of His Flesh, and of His Bones,' [2] and we know that God will hear the voice of His own Son.

Yet this sense of membership in Christ must be developed, not merely at the times of prayer ;

[1] Eph. i. 6.　　　　　　[2] Eph. v 30.

I

it must be the effort of our daily life, the aim of our self-discipline. For it is on this that our Lord's promise depends: 'If ye abide in Me, and My words abide in you, ye shall ask what ye will, and it shall be done unto you.'[1] And as Members of Christ we have the assistance of the Holy Spirit, 'who helpeth our infirmities.' We kneel down, but, notwithstanding all our watchfulness and care, our hearts are cold, and our words come falteringly; but we persevere, and then at times—not always consciously, but at times—we feel the Breath of the Spirit breathing through us and kindling our devotion, and words come to our lips, or longings too great for words well up within our hearts and reach to God. We feel, in one way, that what we say and long for is our own, it has the colour and temper of our minds; but again we feel it is not our own, it is greater and stronger than we are; and then

[1] S. John xv. 7.

we know that it is partly ourselves, partly the Spirit of God, that the music that thrills us is the Breath of the Spirit breathing through the instrument which we have striven so hard to prepare.

Such moments we must cherish and recall in times of darkness ; they enable us to feel and to know that we are not alone in our efforts to pray, but that there is One who helpeth our infirmities, and who, when He sees fit, at any moment can make His power to be felt, though when we are least conscious of it He is still with us.

VII.

THE PRESENCE OF GOD.

THE supreme work of life is the perfect development of character, having ever in view
the Will and purpose of God, the development
of all that God has given to us in relation to
Himself, and the harmonising of all the various
gifts and powers with which we are endowed,
so as to form one perfect whole. Each has to
develop his own personal life, and to resist
all those manifold conflicting claims and forces
that are constantly trying to interfere with it
and to hurt it.

It is scarcely possible for anyone to live
a single day without finding that someone or
something has been intruding upon him in a

way that, if he does not resist it, will more or less injure him.

Other lives and interests cross ours. We may allow ourselves to get entangled by a thousand claims and occupations which are not really any concern of ours. Things constantly press forward and solicit our interference, in which no duty compels us to interfere. On all sides multitudes of things, sometimes the veriest trifles, sometimes matters of greater moment, seem arrayed against us, for no purpose apparently but to dissipate our powers and prevent the concentration and growth of our life.

It is not, indeed, easy for the most conscientious always to know where to draw the line, or to see what is an intrusion and what is a duty ; when to hold aloof and let things of interest pass by, and when to take part in them ; what is the claim of charity, and what is the mere fussiness of pride.

It is, therefore, of the utmost importance that we should know how to protect ourselves from all these distractions, and how to deal with the various circumstances with which we come in contact, in such a way as to force them to help and develop our true life, not to hinder it.

There are, however, two dangers which we must be on our guard against, two wrong ways of meeting these difficulties.

1. No one will ever develop his best self by always watching himself. There are some people who go through life wrapped in a kind of garment of spiritual self-consciousness. They never for a moment forget themselves and their own spiritual state; they are so afraid of being hurt by life, that, in their effort after self-protection, they inflict a fatal injury upon themselves which puts a stop to any healthy growth. They become morbid, intro-spective, timid scrupulous; there is nothing

spontaneous, nothing inspiring in their lives.
They hold themselves back from all those
experiences through which alone it is possible
that life and character should develop, seeking
to protect themselves sometimes at the expense
of definite obligations. They fail to see that in
neglecting to be responsive and sympathetic
they leave the richest side of their own
nature stunted and maimed. For God has so
ordered it that our lives are bound up with one
another, and in neglecting the claims of charity
and the calls of duty we injure ourselves. All
these duties and interests have their danger,
no doubt, but in timidly shrinking from the
dangers that duty involves, we fly into greater
danger, for a life that has turned in upon itself
and is always watching its own growth, or lack of
growth, has already contracted a deadly disease.
No, the atmosphere of spiritual self-consciousness and introspection is not the shelter which

the soul is to find against the distracting interferences of life.

2. But there is another danger. We must not, on the other hand, let ourselves go with undisciplined freedom. There are those who delight in feeling the play of life's many interests and sympathies upon them. With them there is no reserve, no self-restraint, but a constant outpouring of sympathy and activity; rightly revolting against the narrow, inexpansive self-consciousness of some so-called religious people, they go into the other extreme, and pour themselves out upon everyone and everything that interests them. Everything leaves its mark upon their impressionable natures. Finally we feel that it only needs time and sufficiently strong influences to destroy every marked token of individuality in such people, and to exhaust all the gifts with which they began life.

Character certainly does not ripen to its perfection in an atmosphere of general benevolence and undisciplined sympathy, nor will the soul find its shelter in such a self-forgetfulness as that.

Shall we, then, tell the former class of persons that they must get out of themselves by throwing themselves in a spirit of self-abandonment into the lives and interests of others, and the latter that they must hold themselves back and check the outgoings of their sympathy, and try to harden themselves against that sensitive appreciation which exposes them to so much danger ? Undoubtedly they must do this to a certain extent, but they will not find in such an endeavour the real remedy for their fault.

No, there is a better way ; let each try to live in that atmosphere which will at once protect and develop his life ; enabling him to

keep the balance between the twofold claim
from within and from without, yielding himself
to the circumstances and influences that de-
mand his sympathy, yet never losing hold of
himself, and living the inner life without self-
contemplation or the fear to go forth wherever
and whenever duty calls.

The earth in its orbit round the sun passes
through many thousands of miles, yet those
who live upon it are not conscious of any
sudden and great changes, for it bears its own
atmosphere about with it. And as we pass
from one place and occupation to another,
we need to carry our own atmosphere with
us to protect and develop our lives. How shall
we do this ? What kind of atmosphere should
we be wrapped in ? How shall we pass from
prayer to pleasure, from silence into crowded
places, without jar or loss ? How shall we practise watchfulness without becoming morbidly

introspective, or large-hearted and generous
charity, and sensitiveness that both feels and
begets sympathy, without wasting ourselves?
How shall we be able constantly ' to go in and
out and find pasture,' to shelter ourselves from
the rude intrusions that would spoil our lives,
and yet never fail to go forth with our whole
nature alive to every proper claim of the ever-
widening world that asks our help.

There is one sure way. By living more and
more in that atmosphere which draws out all
the powers of the soul, which necessitates its
growth, and in which at the same time it finds
protection from every breath that would blight or
stunt it, which intensifies all its sympathies, and
enables it to see all things in their true proportion.
And that atmosphere is the Presence of God.

The soul that has learnt to shelter itself in
that Presence has gained the protection which
it needs, from itself on the one hand, and, on

the other, from the crowding appeals of life. In that Presence there can be no morbidness, for it is the very Truth ; no stagnation, for it is the Fountain of Life ; no timid holding back from the true claims of life, for that Presence itself bids the soul go forth to work and action.   Nor, on the other hand, can one who lives in that Presence fritter away his life upon things that have no claim upon him, for it ever holds back as well as sends forward.   He who lives beneath its shelter knows full well that the light and protection is limited to the sphere of duty and right, and that if he goes beyond that he must leave it ; but within that sphere he is safe amidst all the noise and distraction and wearying strain of life.   'Thou art a place to hide me in ; Thou shalt preserve me from trouble ; Thou shalt compass me about with songs of deliverance.'[1]   'Thou shalt hide them

[1] Psalm xxxii. 8.

privily in Thine own Presence from the provok-
ing of all men ; Thou shalt keep them secretly
in Thy tabernacle from the strife of tongues!'' [1]

In proportion as we gain the sense of God's
Presence we are safe in the very tumult of life,
in the very thick of the strife of tongues. For
this Presence protects our own individuality ;
it protects us so that we do not lose ourselves,
and become, as we are often apt to do, almost
a mechanical part of the world and the society
in which we live ; sinking into a routine in
which we lose more and more the sense of
responsibility. We certainly need this, a clear
and ever-deepening sense of our own separate
and solitary individuality, with all its consciousness of personal responsibility and the dignity
of personal life. And the first thing that the
realisation of God's Presence does for any man
is to deepen this sense of his own personality

[1] Psalm xxxi. 22.

and responsibility. He lives in a Presence which is stronger than all the influences round him; that Presence isolates him, frees him from the tyranny of the standards and judgments of the little coteries which make his world, and gives him new standards to judge himself by.

Many of those who have the capacities for influencing others, if only they could stand a little apart and be firm, are simply carried hither and thither by the babel of opinion in which they live, and give themselves no time to pause and ask what it is all worth, and what is their own duty; they have formed no clear idea of themselves, no notion of something definite which they were intended to be and to do. Having no strong convictions, they are borne hither and thither by the society in which for the moment they may happen to be.

And when such a person wakens up to realise the Presence of God instantly there follows the

quickened sense of his own personality and
responsibility ; he is wrapped around and
stands alone in that Presence which forces him
to pass judgment upon himself. He sees himself in the Presence of One who knows him,
and has been the silent witness of all he has ever
said or done ; he is compelled to gather himself
out of the multitude, and the full recognition of
his own personal responsibility is forced upon him.
There has come upon him something stronger
than any of those influences which hitherto have
acted upon him, robbing him almost of all
sense of personality, and now he is able to stand
alone, and to withstand what before seemed
impossible. 'Thou art a place to hide me in ;
Thou shalt compass me about with songs of
deliverance.'

There is something very wonderful in the
way in which the thought of God at once
wakens up the dormant or half-lost sense of

one's own personality and the responsibilities that it involves. We cannot come near to Him without realising more deeply ourselves. When Isaiah saw His glory, his first words were, ' Woe is me, for I am undone, because I am a man of unclean lips ; for mine eyes have seen the King, the Lord of hosts !'[1] Made as we are in the Image of God, there is an instinctive rising up to compare ourselves with Him who is the source of our life and our Archetype.

This realisation of God's Presence is the power that gives such an intense personality to many who naturally would not be strong enough to stand alone. Encircled by this Presence, they present that wonderful combination of sensitive timidity and moral courage which belongs to the Christian alone. This is the way men and women who are not by nature strong or independent, but who cling much to others and depend much upon other's judgment,

[1] Isaiah vi. 5.

yet when occasion demands are able quietly to go and do their work in the face of adverse criticism and misunderstanding, for their lives are strong and self-possessed, living in the Presence of Him to whom they are responsible. Amidst all the pain which they may have to suffer, they verily have a 'joy which no man taketh from them.'[1] The Presence of God is thus a shelter and protection for those whose duties compel them to live amidst many distractions and much variety of circumstances. It is as when one goes into a crowded room, and on all sides one hears a babel of voices and sees a multitude of people, one feels oneself lost in the presence of so many; and there amongst them you see one who is very dear to you, and as you draw near to him and hear his voice it seems as if you were leaving all that noisy crowd in the distance, and the tones of his voice at last so

[1] S. John xvi. 22.

K

absorb you that they silence all else, and the
tumult has ceased, and you and he are alone.
'Thou shalt hide them privily in Thy Presence
from the strife of tongues'; and this the Presence
of God can do for us. We can withdraw ourselves
at any moment when we feel ourselves getting
lost, as it were, in a crowded life, and rest under
the shelter of His Presence.

In this way we may protect our life from
dissipating its powers, and from losing itself
amidst the distractions into which duty or
pleasure may call us. 'The name of the Lord is
a strong tower: the righteous runneth into it
and is safe.'[1]

But, on the other hand, the practise of the
Presence of God will be the remedy for those
whose danger is to hold aloof from duties and
to become spiritually self-centred.

For the Presence of God at once lifts one

[1] Prov. xviii. 10.

out of oneself, yet not in such a way as to leave one in ignorance of one's faults ; one sees oneself indeed, one knows oneself in a far truer way than by any amount of introspection, but one sees oneself without self-contemplation and without self-depreciation. Living in a constant spirit of self-watching and self-analysis, one may be quite possibly measuring oneself by false standards ; perhaps by the ideal one's own pride has drawn for one, perhaps by the standard of some other's life, one may be striving after what God never meant and never gave one the power to attain. But as we learn to live in the Presence of God all this becomes impossible ; in the Presence of the Truth we are forced to be true, and it is astonishing to see how those whose aims were very lofty and very unreal, and who had got into an altogether false method of weighing the value of spiritual things, gradually, as they strove to live more in

God's Presence, took a wholly different and truer estimate of life, and thought less and talked less about their own spiritual life. 'Thou requirest truth in the inward parts, and shalt make me to understand wisdom secretly.'[1] They unconsciously gained another standard as they lived more simply before God. They grew out of a timid life of self-analysis into a strong life, in which they saw themselves as God would have them to be. Yet their self-knowledge became, in fact, far deeper and truer.

Certainly, if we need protection from life's many distractions and calls, we need perhaps even more protection from that ever-present atmosphere of self-consciousness which clings around so many like a damp fog ; and not by any means the least dangerous form is spiritual self-consciousness. And we cannot get out of

[1] Psalm li. 6.

this by merely struggling with it, as we might struggle with temper or pride ; such efforts seem often only to rivet the bonds more tightly upon us. We can only get out of it by losing ourselves in another, and there is but one other whose Presence we can always have and never weary, and who will never harm us.

But we must not expect that we shall be able to gain such a protecting sense of God's Presence in a moment. It will be the result of much prayer and mental discipline. We must not be discouraged, therefore, if after a long time we still find that we have made but little progress. " In His Presence is the fulness of joy ; and at His Right Hand there is pleasure for evermore.'[1] The fulness of joy and such lasting pleasure are not to be easily gained ; they are to be won only by those who work hard and suffer much for it.

[1] Psalm xvi. 12.

A few suggestions may be helpful to those who are beginning the practise of the Presence of God.

1. The mind must be kept in a healthy state; if it becomes overstrained, it will never be able to attain to the power of resting in God's Presence. The realising of the Presence of God is not to be by a straining of the mind, or by a forcing of the imagination; the soul must grow into it gradually; it must be a rest, not a weariness. Any time, therefore, that the mind feels strained or wearied, it should be relaxed; we should turn to something else, and give it rest. We may test our progress by the growing sense of liberty, the facility and freedom from scruple or anxiety with which the mind rests itself when it feels the danger of strain or weariness; scruple and fear and a burden of rules will make advance in this practice impossible.

2. Do not be anxious to grow too fast. If

you are impatient and overtax your strength, you will fail altogether. To live in God's Presence means to be very holy, and, there-fore, to grow in the sense of His Presence means growth in holiness. It is one of the chief fruits of a holy life, and we cannot see that fruit except as the life grows and deepens. One part, so to speak, of the spiritual life cannot outstrip all the rest; be patient, therefore, and be content to grow slowly. It is good, indeed, never to forget the Presence of God for a moment, but it would be fatal to begin by even trying to keep the mind always concentrated. 'When I was a child I thought as a child.' Begin by recalling the thought of God's Presence at certain times, by ejaculation, by setting apart a few minutes once or twice in the day to remain quietly wrapping yourself round with the thought, and be content with this till you are spiritually able for more.   The evil results of lack of prudence, which is often lack of humility, will not be healed by grace.

3. In work that should occupy the mind give your mind to it.   Offer it to God when you begin and when you finish it.   But while at work you must seek to glorify God by using all the powers of your mind in what you are doing.   Therefore do not try to realise God's Presence at such times, except it may be in a moment's pause, but let the conscious thought of His glory stimulate you to do your best.

4. Build the practise of the Presence of God upon the 'indwelling Presence of Christ.' Let each communion remind you what you are as a Christian—a Member of Christ, fed by His Life.   Let each communion intensify the realisation of that ever-abiding Presence within you, and let the thought of each communion remain with you till your next, even if through

no fault of yours a long period intervenes.
Some may seek to place themselves in the
Presence of God as in an atmosphere of holy
light wrapping them round—that luminous
'shadow of the Almighty' of which the
Psalmist speaks; but it will be perhaps an
easier, certainly a surer and a quicker road to
holiness to turn within, and to rest oneself
upon that heavenly light that burns in the
inmost depth of the soul, radiating forth upon
all its powers and faculties, the Shekinah of the
Divine Presence. 'In the secret place of His
dwelling shall He hide me, and set me up upon
a rock of stone.'[1]

[1] Psalm xxvii.

VIII.

THE HIDDEN LIFE.

THERE were two sides to the life of our Lord. To those who saw Him in His public ministry during the last three years of His life, it seemed one of constant and unceasing labour. He 'went about doing good.'[1] He was ever at the call of any who needed Him; He gave Himself no rest, so that He had not so much time as to eat bread. As we read the Gospels, we read of days crowded with work of the most trying kind, dealing constantly with all sorts of people, addressing crowds and then meeting the needs of individuals, and never apparently alone, the Apostles always with Him. His life was almost lived in public. Almost the

[1] Acts x. 38.

whole Gospel is taken up with the events of about three years. To those who saw Him and heard Him, it was as if His life seemed to be without rest, a life of unsparing energy and toil.

But there was another side which they could not see—the hidden life. His public life was built upon and rested upon a life of thirty years of hiddenness and preparation. For every year in public there were ten years in private. In the solitude and retirement of Nazareth He grew up ; there His human character formed and developed, far from the noise and excitement of the world ; thirty years out of thirty-three He lived there, almost His whole life. What does three years count for in many a man's life? And He spent His whole life except three years at Nazareth.

And even after that long period of preparation, He retired into deeper solitude before His public ministry began. He spent forty days in the wilderness in absolute solitude, except for the presence of visiturs from the world of spirits. And again and again we read of His withdrawing in the midst of His life of active work for prayer. 'In the morning, rising up a great while before day, He went out and departed into a solitary place, and there prayed.'[1]

Yes, there was the hidden life from which the public life gained all its power. All His actions were rooted in God ; He never forgot Himself, never got carried away by the interest or excitement of the multitudes with whom He had to deal, never swerved from the purpose and Will of God.

The hidden life *is* hidden, we know almost nothing about it ; if it were known, and could be described, it would not be hidden. Now

[1] S. Mark ii. 35.

and again, in the thick and pressure of His
work, the veil is lifted for a moment, and we
are allowed to see those nights of prayer ; but
men could feel and see the mysterious power
in His words and acts and bearing that were
the outward manifestations of that inner life,
but that was all. His life—that out of which
all this public life grew—was hidden.

It is the same with the Body of Christ—the
Church. It has its public life ; we read of it in
history, we see it to-day. The Church, everywhere in all the world's busiest places, teaching,
mingling with all the thought and interests of
the day, struggling against opposition, dealing with sin and suffering and misery, never
resting, pressing forward into new fields of
conquest, beset with temporal needs which
have to be met. How is it to live and grow in
such scenes ? How, amidst the strain and
pressure that is upon it on all sides, is it to

keep true to God? There are so many induce-ments to compromise and to advance by worldly methods ; so little time to collect itself and to meet the requirements of a new age. What is to support it? What gives it that power so far beyond its number and the influence of its individual members? It, too, must have its hidden life upon which it rests, from which it draws its succours, by which it preserves its strength.

It is now, like our Lord, in its public life pressed and driven, and beset, like Him, by the needy multitude and by its many antagonists ; but its life is not merely what is seen and heard : it has another life which cannot be seen nor measured, but upon which it depends for all its power, from which it draws all the secret of its strange influence. The Church, if it is to live, must have its hidden life of prayer and fasting and solitude.

The Church is one Body composed of many members. *All* men are bound to one another by the tie of a common nature, but Christians are bound by a twofold tie, the tie of a common nature and of membership in Christ : 'For by one Spirit are we all baptized into one Body'[1] And it follows that the Church can live one part of her life through some of her members and another part through others, for so closely are all the members bound together in one Body that, as St. Paul says, 'if one member suffer, all the members suffer with it ; or one member be honoured, all the members rejoice with it.'[2]

Therefore, as the different members of the body have their different functions and work for the edification of the body, so in the Body of Christ all have not the same office ; there is a division of labour amongst the members, but it is for the life of the Body. Thus the

[1] 1 Cor. xii. 13.　　　[2] 1 Cor. xii. 26.

Church goes forth into the world through some ; through others she keeps up that hidden life which is her strength. The work of some is seen and heard and attracts notice ; it is done, as our Lord's works in His ministry were done, before the world. The work of others is not seen, it is only felt.

Just as in the natural body we can see a man working and hear him speak, but we cannot see the processes by which the body is nourished and life preserved, for all the work of preserving and strengthening the life is un-seen. So in the Body of Christ, the develop-ment of its inner strength, the preservation and growth of its life, is hidden. Behind all the movements of its activity is the hidden life from which it draws its power. 'Are all apostles, are all prophets, are all teachers ; do all speak with tongues?'[1] There are

[1] 1 Cor. xii. 29.

all over the world, many, of whom men know little or nothing, who are the fountains of the Church's strength. How strange they are, those lives of constant suffering : men and women who seem cast aside and useless, tied down to sick-beds, it may be with bodies paralyzed or enfeebled so that they cannot work ; some strong man stricken down in his prime and doomed to years of lingering illness and wasting strength. What use can such lives be except to try the patience of those who have to tend them ? But no ; they little know themselves that it is upon such lives as theirs that the Church depends for power to bear up against the world and to prosecute her missionary labours. If on one side there is a great putting forth of strength, there must be on the other a proportionate building up and nourishment, or the life will be soon exhausted.

So in one way or another God will surely call

people to the life of retirement and prayer or suffering in proportion as the demands upon the Church become more exacting. The call may take many forms, and perhaps different forms in different ages, but such calls are surely given. Sometimes it may be in a most un-obtrusive way. A person is kept back time after time from the opportunity of doing active work. How often has a young woman in her own home looked forward to devoting herself to some work, perhaps she has had it in her mind for years, and believed God was calling her to it; but every time, just as the opportunity seemed to come, the door was closed in her face: some clear call of duty, sickness, the care of those who depended upon her, one thing or another always stopped the way and threw her back. It seemed to her a puzzle that God should appear to call and not give the power to correspond; but it may be, though she felt the call, she mistook its meaning, and God was leading her on unconsciously to fulfil it. She was thrown back upon prayer; her longing to help others needed some vent, and she found it in intercession; then she passed on from intercessory prayers to intercessory acts, till her life was one of constant sacrifice for those whom she was apparently held back from helping. Her vocation was to the hidden life; no one ever noticed it, least of all herself. For 'her life was hidden with Christ in God.'[1]

Or it may be a priest, full of zeal for souls, and with great missionary gifts, struck down a few years after his ordination, and, as people said, a most promising and useful life put an end to. And yet, as years went by, those who knew him best saw another life grow and spring up amidst the ruins of the old one; as one sees the bud form under the dead leaf of autumn;

[1] Col. iii. 3.

none of the zeal had been lost, none of the love for souls, none of the sacerdotal spirit, but it had been purified and redirected into the offering of a better sacrifice than service, the sacrifice of himself. He had grasped more and more the mystery of vicarious suffering, and his life went up in one unending sacrifice and oblation for those whom in act he was prevented from helping.

Or again, that multitude of lives in no way marked, which as time goes on get mellowed and softened by age, and perhaps by the ordinary disappointments of life, from whom most of the world's attractions has long since passed, and in their place has come a growing love to God and a desire to do something for others before they die to atone for a selfish, aimless life. From how many such there goes up before God a constant stream of prayer and acts, many of them enforced acts of self-denial, and often intense inward suffering borne with fortitude and in silence ; the world has gone from them and heaven has not come, the remnants of old worldly ways still cling to them which they hate, causing them bitter humiliations, their place in very truth knows them no more, and still with all there is a pathetic effort to lay hold on God with minds dulled and heavy, and to keep up their interest in the world by praying for it. Surely such lives have power, and such prayers, joyless strugglings after an unseen God, are not rejected ; and truly such lives are hidden, for few are sufficiently interested in them to remark them.

But, above all, the hidden life of the Church is to be found in the cloister, amongst those whose vocation is primarily—in many cases only—to a life of prayer. Behind all the active life of the Church stand those great religious orders devoted to prayer and penitence, witnessing to the world that Christianity is not merely a philanthropic society, but that it is devotion to a Person. These men and women devote themselves not to active work for their brethren—in many cases they shut themselves out from the possibility of any such work—but believing that the closer they are to God the more real help they can bring to the world, they give up everything else that they may draw ever closer to Him. As they approach Him, and their lives are more united to Him, their sympathies become enlarged, for their hearts are close to the Heart of the world's Redeemer. All interests but His die out, but all that is dear to Him becomes the absorbing passion of their souls. They are able to enter as few others into His sympathies, to long with His longing for the salvation of souls, to enter with opening vision into the mystery of the atonement and redemption till they yearn to partake in some measure of His sufferings, to suffer with Him for others' sins. They realise something of the reality of the unity of the Body of Christ and of the power of vicarious suffering. Who can tell of the power that from age to age has gone forth from these unknown lives? men and women literally buried out of the world's sight and knowledge, who, while the world has gone on its way and enjoyed itself, and often sneered at the selfish lives of those who fled from it to save their own souls, little knew that they were the world's saviours, whose lives are a living sacrifice for their brethren.

Yes, the Church has her hidden life, the secret of her power, the unseen fountains of her strength. If the Church's life were only what men gauged it by and applauded it for—what they could see and measure by results gained and assured—if that were all, that must soon exhaust itself and fail. But there *is* another side, its true strength, which many count as waste of strength, ' All that the world's coarse thumb and finger cannot plumb,' the life hidden with Christ in God.

And as with our Lord and His Body, so with the individual soul. Everyone has the outer life and the inner life, the life which is lived before the world and the life which none can see but God. To some the outer life is the main thing ; they think little of the hidden life, they would gladly not think of it at all. To others the hidden life is the first, the chief consideration of all ; it is that for which they live, it is from its springs that they draw their strength, it is for its sake that the most real sacrifices are made. Yet the most hopelessly superficial person has his hidden life—that inner life of compromises with conscience, of breaking down barriers that God has set up between the soul and sin ; of secrets that it has with itself, which none shall ever know of, things done which it will not allow even itself to face and to acknowledge ; of memories driven off into dark corners of the soul which come out at night like ghosts and haunt it ; of a deepening sense of dissatisfaction and of unfulfilled possibilities—of a noble ideal of life that once was possible, but now only returns to waken remorse and bitterness. And then there is the growing feeling which always comes to such people sooner or later, that matters are passing out of their own hands, that currents are setting in one direction so fast that they cannot be controlled, that life has taken things into its own hands since the will has not taken the trouble to control them, and that all real liberty is gone. Yes, the most superficial, the most utterly frivolous person, who seems to have no higher thought than the enjoyment of the moment's pleasure, has a hidden life, and I do not think it would be true to call it shallow ; it has, indeed, an infinite depth, it is the beginning of the thirst that shall never be quenched.

Such is possibly the inner state of many who do not cultivate the hidden life. For it needs to be cultivated. The tendency of most natures is to begin by turning outwards. The life of the infant begins with the senses, the claims of duty constantly call us out, the pressure of the outer life is enormous. A firm exercise of the will is needed to call the soul back into itself, that it may dwell within rather than without. It has but to let itself go, to take no trouble with itself, to practise no self-discipline, and it will drift further and further into the life of the senses, and get ever more entangled in external things.

But the true hidden life is not a mere holding back of the powers of the soul. No life is mere repression. It is possible to have one's life turned inward to its own destruction. There is the danger of self-absorption and self-contemplation which has to be constantly guarded against, for a soul whose inner life is merely or mostly self-contemplation, is in a far worse state than one which lives a wholly external life. The hidden life is not to be a life of self-analysis and self-torturing, but the very reverse—a life that is deeply interior, yet with an entire self-forgetfulness.

What, then, is the source and meaning of the hidden life of the Christian? It is based upon those words of St. Paul, ' I live, yet not I, but Christ liveth in me;'[1] 'Christ in you, the hope of glory.'[2] It is rooted in the soul's union with Christ. It grows out of the fact that in baptism we are 'made members of his Body,'[3] that 'all our fresh-springs hence-

---

[1] Gal. ii. 20.   [2] Col. i. 27.   [3] Eph. v. 30.

forth are to be in Him.'[1] The soul which is striving to develop the hidden life turns inward, not in self-contemplation but to contemplate and to develop its union with Christ. It bears about this sacred Presence with it wherever it goes ; it becomes increasingly conscious of a power within that is not its own, yet that is wholly at its disposal. It feels a growing strength, not the strength of its own natural gifts, but quite apart from all that it has naturally ; it understands the meaning of St. Paul's paradox, 'When I am weak, then am I strong';[2] it perceives its own weakness only too clearly, but it finds a power not its own which flows into it as it throws itself more and more upon the indwelling Presence of Christ.

This Presence then, within each baptized Christian, is the source of its hidden life ; upon this it is built ; the practise of the hidden life

[1] Psalm lxxxvii. 7.   [2] 2 Cor. xii. 10.

depends upon the development of all that results from it, the using of the powers that flow from it. For though we have, every one of us, this great gift, its action depends upon our faith and upon our will. To many it is but a treasure hidden in the field ; they weary themselves in the ploughing and harrowing and sowing upon the surface of their nature, while the true source of their riches lies buried deep down within them.

If we would avoid the danger on the one hand of living wholly external lives and wasting our strength, and on the other hand of becoming self-centred or morbidly intro-spective, we must strive to live the hidden life, to find the roots of our life running down into His, from whom comes our strength. All that helps towards this will be in the end a blessing. Temptations that we have fought and failed to overcome for years may at last drive us to the one true source of power, drive us into ourselves to seek the power hidden there. Prayers that never seem to bring us nearer to God may at last lead us, if I may use such an expression, not so much to pray ourselves as to be silent and listen to Christ praying within us. The hopelessness that comes from the memory of past sins and wasted years, and gifts undeveloped, may drive us, not to look to a Mediator upon the throne of God merely, but to the realisation that we need more, more than One standing at God's right hand to intercede for us, even the Presence of that Mediatorial life within ourselves, our own living membership in Him who is the Mediator. Yes, and if God is merciful to us, we shall feel the spring and movements of that new life amidst the decay and death of the old, rising up like a fountain and fertilising the barren soil, and making the wilderness to blossom as the rose ; out of the despair of nature will spring the dawn of the hope of grace, out of weakness strength.

This is the secret of the saints, this was the source of their power, this it was that puzzled men as they watched them : they could not see the source of that strength by which they were enabled to overcome the world, their power was so far in excess of their natural gifts ; no, for ' their life was hidden with Christ in God.'

IX.

TWO CHIEF ACTS OF THE SOUL.

THE whole Christian life may be summed up in two acts—coming to Christ, and abiding in Christ.

Everyone that has lost his baptismal innocency, if he will save his soul has to come back to our Lord. Each has his own history, his own experience of all that this means. God leads different souls in different ways; some, no doubt, have stopped suddenly in a life of alienation and in a moment have turned and begun to trace their steps back; with others the process has been so slow and gradual that they can scarcely tell where or how it began. There was a growing discontent with their life, a deepening desire for better things, struggles often—most often—ending in failure, efforts to pray, a sense of weakness and of sin, a gradual movement accompanied by many relapses, which ended in the soul finding itself turned and facing Godward.

Some have felt sensibly in all this process a marked and conscious action of God's Grace, a sense of the divine assistance that at times seemed almost irresistible, making everything easy, and seeming to lift the soul out of the reach of its old temptations and habits. With others it has been different; there has been from moment to moment little sense of God's assistance or of His love, only the consciousness of the hand-to-hand struggle with sin and of the difficulties to be overcome. The experience of one is not the experience of another; God delights to deal with each in His own way as He sees to be best, and much harm is done by

M

pressing personal experience into the sphere of dogma, and trying to urge our own experiences upon others. It is only as they look back, it may be after many years, that they are able to say, ' If the Lord Himself had not been on our side, when men rose up against us, they had swallowed us up quick, when they were so wrathfully displeased at us ; but praised be the Lord who hath not given us over for a prey unto their teeth : our soul is escaped, even as a bird out of the snare of the fowler ; the snare is broken, and we are delivered.'

There are two sides to all the actions of our Christian life—the work of our own will and of the grace of God. God cannot work in us apart from our own co-operation, and all our most strenuous endeavours must fail without the assistance of His grace. Some are more conscious of one side, some of the other, though in all both the human and the divine must co-operate. St. Paul brings the two sides together when he says, 'Work out your own salvation, for it is God that worketh in you.' Our Lord teaches both sides when He says, 'No man cometh unto Me except the Father which hath sent Me draw him;' and again, 'I, if I be lifted up, will draw all men unto Me.' Here He teaches us the action of God upon the soul, but He says again, 'Come unto Me, all ye that labour and are heavy-laden, and I will give you rest.' Here He appeals to the soul; the coming must be its own act. It is not to be wondered at that some ardent natures are most conscious of the drawing, while others feel most the action of their own will; the experiences of both are true to the teaching of Scripture, but each has felt one side so strongly that he has not been always conscious of the other.

Now the coming to Christ is not by a movement of the body but of the mind; it is the entering into a certain relationship with a Person. We know how quickly we may travel away from one whom we have loved; it is not so easy to return. Not many days after the prodigal's breach with his father he was in a far country; it took him a long time to get back. Two persons may be living side by side and gradually drifting further apart though they are constantly in one another's company. A husband and wife, bound by God in that mystical union which makes ' them twain to be one flesh,' may nevertheless be as far apart as the poles. Two friends who had no interest apart one from the other a few days ago, may find that some little jar or slight misunderstanding makes it impossible to give or take sympathy to-day; the voice that was so full of kindness seems to have lost its true ring. A separation has begun. Often, indeed, the closer and more intimate the friendship the quicker and more complete the separation when once it begins; it is easier to make up a quarrel with a mere acquaintance than with a dear friend.

Thus there are constant movements of heart and mind without any bodily movements; in a day, in an hour, the heart and mind and will may have gone a long journey. The drawing near of two friends or their separation is like nothing else. It is the mysterious action of one person upon another. How different it is from a merely intellectual process. You have read and inquired as much as possible about some well-known person; you know what he has done and said, and to a large extent you can understand the tone of his mind on most subjects, and you have made up your own mind about him—you do not like him; yet five minutes in his company changes your whole feeling towards him; you

have come directly in contact with his person,
and through a hundred channels he lets in upon
you a knowledge of himself that you never
could gain in any other way. You ask yourself what has made you change your mind;
has he argued away your prejudice, has he
answered the objections you had to his con-
duct? No; he has not even referred to them.
The fact is, you had previously only an
intellectual knowledge *about* him, now you
know *himself*; that subtle thing, a personal
life, has flowed in upon you through no one
channel but through many, and the conclu-
sions of one part of your nature are corrected
or balanced by those of another. What a
journey you have taken in those five minutes
from the time when you held aloof from
him on your first meeting to the time—a
few minutes after—when you felt prejudice, dislike, antagonism, all give way,

and you let yourself go out towards him,
saying, 'I like him.' This is the 'coming'
of one person to another, the only personal drawing near, not of the body but of
the self.

And this is but an illustration of the
soul's coming to Christ; it is the coming to a
Person in such a way as only one person can
come to another, the bringing oneself under
and surrendering oneself to a personal influence.
It does not consist in a great deal of knowledge
about Him, but in knowing *Him*; indeed, many
have come knowing very little about Him,
learning all that was to be known from Himself.
Nathanael came full of prejudice and with
strong biblical arguments against what Philip
had told him of his claims. Two sentences
from our Lord's own lips sweep away all the
arguments and prejudices, and bring him to
His feet with a profession of faith like S.

Peter's : 'Thou art the Son of God, Thou art the king of Israel.'[1]

In the formation of any friendship two persons have to be considered ; there may be obstacles, or lack of sympathy, or misunderstanding on both sides, or one may be most anxious for a friendship from which the other holds back. The friendship does not depend merely upon the efforts of one. But in drawing near to Christ we know that there are no obstacles on His side. No ; He has not to be won round, He is the suppliant ; the hindrances, prejudice, dislike, ignorance, are all on our side. If only we remove them we shall find how close He is to us. We have taken our journey into a far country of moral alienation, we care for, are interested in, perhaps live wholly absorbed in things which are hateful to Him, and we are injuring the

[1] S. John i. 49.

work for which He gave His life. However near we may be to Him outwardly, we are worlds apart from Him in heart and will, and the return must be by the effort to get into moral sympathy, the struggle to do right, the determination at any rate to be in earnest. He who longs and strives to be good has already created a bond of sympathy with Christ, has returned, indeed, a long way towards Him. As one after another of those barriers which we have set up in ourselves are removed, the light and love come streaming in, and the bonds of that mystical friendship become woven which grow stronger through eternity.

It is a wonderful experience which the soul gains in that journey which consists not in traversing space, but in a moral approach, a turning of the mind to contemplate and the will to choose and, at last, of the heart to love what Christ loves, and then finding behind all this the living, loving Person who reveals Himself.

The first act of the soul, then, is the coming to Christ ; though this in one sense never ends, for it is ever drawing nearer as it grows in holiness and admits more and more of His knowledge and love.

The other act is the abiding in Him. Having drawn near it must abide—it is always more difficult to be passive than active, the very effort in coming, the consciousness of meeting and overcoming difficulties, strengthens and encourages the soul ; but to abide—there is where so many fail. Many of those who have drawn near turn aside and walk no more with Him—unable to persevere. Only he that is 'faithful unto death shall receive the crown of life.'[1]   The life of the saints in heaven is the

[1] Rev. ii. 10.

eternal abiding in Him to whom they came here on earth.

Now the abiding in Christ involves three things.

1. First, negatively the giving up of everything that hinders this union. After the first great surrender of what is positively sinful, no rule can be laid down which is applicable to every one. There are many things that are harmless in themselves that some feel obliged to give up if they would abide in Christ ; there are things, indeed, that may be helpful to one which would be a hindrance to another. We cannot lay down arbitrary rules as to what is necessary to be given up in the way of pleasure, or relaxation, or self-indulgence ; the wisest guide will, I believe, leave each to take the initiative as to what he must and must not do. It would be a fatal thing to begin by exacting too much. Who can tell how God intends to lead another ?

All that the wisest can do is to point out what seems to be God's leading. The fact that I feel obliged to deal very sternly with myself does not necessarily involve that another should. A pleasure that would be wrong for me might be very good for another. Many a person might say with perfect truth, I cannot give up such and such a thing, I do not love God sufficiently to do without it, my life would be too empty, it does not in any way come between me and God at present. No; in the earlier stages of the spiritual life it would not be true to say that God was all in all to one: there are doubtless various portions of one's life which God has not yet won to Himself, and these are filled up by pursuits and interests which, so far, do not interfere with God's hold upon the soul ; the soul, so far as it knows God, is abiding in Him.

There is a better way of leading men onward; it is the way of nature as well as the

way of grace—positively rather than negatively.
I ask you as you begin to serve God to make but
one rule—to give up all that you are conscious of
hindering your union with Him.   As you get to
know Him better He will become more exacting
in His demands; you will find that many things
which now are harmless and in a measure necessary
to you will begin to interfere with your union with
God. Resolve that if you find this you will give
them up ; you will be able to do in a few years
what it would be absurd to ask you to do now.
As God comes more into your life and demands
that it should be more emptied of other things,
obey Him and He will reward you by a greater
gift of Himself. The whole pathway of your life
will thus be strewn with various things that you
have abandoned for what is better, things that
once seemed to you necessary to your life. The
advance is a constant self-emptying, but not
that your life may be a void, but to make room

for larger interests, keener pleasures, deeper joys, a more absorbing love. Once you said, 'If the spiritual life means the giving up of this work or companionship, I do not think it would be worth the sacrifice.' 'Very well,' was the answer; 'do not give it up, keep it till you feel that the spiritual life is the love of a Person for whom it is worth giving it up.' Now it is gone, for you have come in sight of what is more worth having. The growth in the spiritual life is thus a constant exchange: first the giving up of what is positively bad for good, then the surrender of things good in themselves for better: 'For brass I will bring gold, and for iron I will bring silver, and for wood brass, and for stones iron.'[1] Such is the promise in the kingdom of the Messias, and at last 'The sun shall be no more thy light by day, neither for brightness shall the moon give light unto thee;

[1] Isaiah lx. 17.

but the Lord shall be unto thee an everlasting light, and thy God thy glory.'[1] Even the sun and moon shall become needless ; in some new and more direct experience of God they shall need nothing to reflect His light, but drink immediately from Himself His strength and inspiration.

This is the meaning of the life of sacrifice ; it has ever before it a positive rather than a negative end, and it aims at life, not death— death only as the gateway to a better life. It looks with no puritan eye of contempt at the fair things that the world has, or at those whose lives are less stern ; it only gives up what it does surrender to gain something better.

'For the power to give up many things— every earthly thing—is at bottom a power of not being able to do without other things. He to whom honour is necessary can do without money. He who must have goodness can get

[1] Isaiah lx. 19.

along without praise. He who must have God's communion can do without the sweet companionship of fellow-men. He who cannot lose his eternity can easily cast aside time and the body which belongs to it, and by the martyr's slow or sudden death exchange the visible for the invisible, the symbol for the reality ; nay, he who values most intensely his friend's or his child's life, can, not easily, but still not grudgingly, let go the joy and daily comfort of his friend's or his child's hourly presence, and see him die that he may enter into life.

' On these two ladders, as it were, by these two seals, the order of human character mounts up—the power to do without and the power not to do without. As you grow better there are some things that are always growing looser in their grasp upon you ; there are other things that are always taking tighter hold upon your life. You sweep up out of the grasp of money, praise, ease, distinction. You sweep up into the necessity of truth, courage, virtue, love, and God. The gravitation of the earth grows weaker, the gravitation of the stars takes stronger and stronger hold upon you. And, on the other hand, as you grow worse, as you go down the terrible opposite of all, this comes to pass. The highest necessities let you go, and the lowest necessities take tighter hold of you. Still, as you go down, you are judged by what you can do without and what you cannot do without. You come down at last where you cannot do without a comfortable dinner and an easy bed, but you can do without an act of charity or a thought of God. The poor sot finds his misery sealed with this double seal, that he cannot miss his glass of liquor, and he can miss without a sigh every good company and virtuous wish.

The abiding in Christ, then, demands a surrender of all that hinders the union of the

N

soul with Him. There is no broad rule that can be laid down beforehand ; it is an individual matter between each soul and Christ. All possibility of pride or harsh criticism of others is out of the question, for none can judge beforehand of what another ought to give up. Each must follow as he is led, resolving that if need be he will give up all for all.

2. But again, the abiding in Christ involves the positive clinging to Him. It is like the growth of a friendship ; at first these two people were very little to one another, but by intercourse and acts of kindness they got to know one another better, then one took more hold upon the thoughts of the other, the influence became stronger, when outwardly separated they were less and less apart in thought. Every faculty of the soul was brought under the influence imagination, memory, affection. So it is with the soul's abiding in Christ ; there is

an ever-growing intimacy and interchange of thought, the mind is more constantly filled with His presence, His influence gradually penetrates through the whole soul, shaping and forming the character. The first question in coming to any decision is, 'What would He wish?' the last question when any work is done is, 'Will it be pleasing to Him?' The whole character is swayed and controlled by His influence. How wonderful it is to see many a rough, undisciplined self-centred man pass beneath the spell of that sacred Presence and gradually become transformed, still, indeed, himself, but all with that unmistakable characteristic that betokens His work.

> ' For good ye are and bad, and like to coins,
> Some true, some light, but every one of you
> Stamped with the image of the King.'

If, then, the soul is abiding in Christ, the mind will be more and more filled with the thought of Him, His influence will be consciously felt in all one does. None can live near Him without becoming like Him.

3. And, once more, the abiding in Christ is not all our own doing. If we are striving to hold fast to Him, we must remember that He is holding us more tightly still in His grasp. We often feel how difficult it is to keep near Him; but have we not felt, too, at times how difficult it is to break away from Him? He will not let us go. There have been times when inwardly we had altogether broken with Him, but He still kept His Hand upon us and drew us back. We have sometimes rebelled at His persistency and felt, 'I wish He would leave me to go my own way.' No, it is not so easy to get free from His grasp; if ever there is a final breach between the soul and Christ, the last hand to loose its hold is His, not ours.

Now, the result of this life of union with

Christ is that it brings forth fruit. 'As the branch cannot bear fruit of itself, except it abide in the vine, no more can ye, except ye abide in M ɔ.'[1] The branch is to be adorned with the fruit of the vine. 'I am the Vine, ye are the branches.' 'He that abideth in Me and I in him, the same bringeth forth much fruit, for apart from Me ye can do nothing.' The soul is to be adorned with the graces of Christ ; it is to show forth virtues that are not its own by nature, but are the result of the action of our Lord's life upon it ; as the sap of the vine circulates through the branch, so is the life of Christ to flow into and to nourish the soul, and this will have visible results, the branch will be laden with the fruit of the vine ; it is unmistakable : ' Of thorns men do not gather figs, nor of a bramble-bush gather they grapes ;'[2] the fruit of the soul will betoken its union with the true vine. This is

[1] S. John xv. 4.   [2] S. Luke vi. 44.

the purpose of all God's dealings with it, that it may bring forth not leaves only but fruit. And for this purpose He prunes it. If it were not for the pruning, much of the sap would be exhausted in bringing forth leaves; but the husbandman prunes it, cutting off much of the over-luxuriant growth, that in the autumn there may be a plenteous harvest of fruit. The result of the pruning is at first a loss of the natural rich and undisciplined growth. The tree has lost under the pruning knife all its beauty, much of its apparent life, but time shows that the husbandman acted wisely when the grapes begin to fill and ripen.

Now our Lord says, 'I am the Vine, and My Father is the Husbandman.' His cause and ours is the same. He is the vine, we the branches, therefore the Father deals with every branch with the same tender care as He has for the vine. To injure the branch is to injure the tree ; we are sure while we abide in the vine that no real harm shall happen unto us, though much that is beautiful and the outcome of the free play of life may need to be pruned away, and though we cannot see the wisdom of much that is done till long after, till the time of the ripening fruit comes.

But all this most people can understand. We all know how much we need to be dealt with and disciplined by one who understands us better than we know ourselves, and whose love is strong enough to take from us those harmful things which we have not the courage to give up ourselves ; if only we can perceive the action of the Husbandman, we are prepared to accept it humbly and patiently. But how many things happen that it seems impossible to trace to the Hand of God, nay, that we can clearly trace to a very different hand, the hand not of love but of hate. How often has the sins of another been the discipline of one's life, sometimes with a refinement of cruelty that seems diabolical. Two persons are bound together in marriage, seemingly to curse and ruin one another. A husband takes pleasure in hurting his wife in every possible way, in throwing every difficulty in her path when she tries to do right, seeking to degrade her and rob her of all self-respect; or a wife makes her husband's life unbearable; how is it possible to attribute such things to God? Many a person says, 'If I could see God's hand in all this, I would try to accept it, but I cannot.'

But we must distinguish between the pruning knife and the hand that holds it; the knife may be forged in hell; there need be neither wisdom nor love in it, but it cannot cut unless someone takes it into his hand. The gardener takes that cruel steel that finds pleasure merely in cutting, and he directs and controls it; it cannot lop off any leaf or any

branch, it can only do the work that it is
directed to do. No, there is no love in it, but
along that sharp edge there trembles the love
and the wisdom of the gardener who uses it.
'Thou couldst have no power at all against Me
except it were given thee from above ;'[1] so said
our Lord to Pilate, whose cowardice and weakness were, as it were, His pruning knife. He
looked not at the knife, but at the hand that held
it. 'My Father is the Husbandman.' If we
try to do this we shall often see the wisdom and
the love that directs and controls the most ruthless
cruelty of another in its action upon our own
life. How her love for her worthless son has
been the scourge of that woman's life ; yes, and
as we look deeper we can see it was to all
human appearance the only thing that could
have brought her to God ; the knife was wisely
guided, though it cut so deep. How that fair

[1] S. John xix. 11.

home was wrecked by that woman's sin, and her husband was so proud of his home, and loved it so ; it was perhaps just the one point on which he could be reached. While the things of earth were so happy he had no thought for the deeper things of life, and the knife cut it all cruelly away, and then in time the fruit began to appear, though for a long time the life looked unshapely and bare, and almost without the power to put itself forth again.

It will be always so ; the Husbandman can use any knife, but He will always act with wisdom and with love. For the pruning is a token that the branch has the possibility of bearing fruit : ' Every branch that beareth fruit He pruneth it, that it may bring forth more fruit.'

Therefore, if the soul has come to Christ and is abiding in Him, it must expect to find the Hand of God upon it. In all that comes upon it, it must look up beyond the mere instrument through which its troubles imme- diately come ; it must look to see the hand that holds and guides the knife, and it must yield itself to the discipline, only longing that its life may be enriched and adorned by the fruit that comes from the branches abiding in the vine.

X.

PERSEVERANCE.

THERE are virtues that are of so strong and independent a nature that they seem able to stand alone and to live on when everything else in the soul that is noble has died. One meets with people sometimes who are corrupt to the heart's core and yet are not wanting in generosity—that one remnant of better days lives on while everything else is gone. Or again, there are people who, while they have lost all the virtues that belong to the gentler side of their nature, and have become hard and bitter and censorious, yet have a very strong and masterful sense of duty ; but as we get to know these people better we shall find that while the form of the virtue remains the substance is practically gone, though, so far as it goes, it is good, but it is rather of nature than of grace. The spendthrift generosity of the prodigal is a very different thing from the Christian grace of charity, still it is, so far as it goes, a virtue, and it is often a surprise and a joy to find how long some such virtues will live on amidst the corruption and evil that is around them.

Then, too, there are virtues that never stand alone, they are of so delicate a texture that they need some other virtue to protect them and upon which they may rest. Purity will nearly always grow, resting upon the prop of humility ; let humility fail, and purity, like some fading flower, will begin to bend earthwards and to lose its bloom ; inward peace twines itself round the strong support of self-oblation ; even moral courage that seems so strong and self-reliant, will gain strength and a firmer root in the soul if it grows upon the tender yet unbending support of penitence; let penitence deepen and moral courage will grow so strong that one who is naturally weak will be ready to face every difficulty and danger; let penitence begin to die, and the will that was so strong and brave becomes cowardly.

Thus there are virtues that seem as it were twin sisters and always grow in pairs, the virtue that seems the more robust often depending for its life upon one in appearance far more delicate. They grow in pairs and they die in pairs. When one begins to droop, the other is sure to droop with it, it cannot stand alone. Self-forgetfulness depends upon the practise of the Presence of God. When the soul has gained this hidden grace it will show upon its outer life that other virtue which everyone must see and admire, yet none can tell upon what a very delicate and hidden support it depends for its extraordinary strength; let the Presence of God grow dim within and the presence of self at once presses to the front.

Thus it often happens that the virtue which we most need and desire is not to be cultivated directly, but through some other virtue that at first sight may seem to have little connexion with it, yet as we watch it growing we shall generally find that the other virtue has twined itself round it, or followed close upon it. We scarcely realise how purity is very often best gained, not by a direct struggle for it, but by striving for humility ; and as humility grows we shall surely find that it has brought with it the grace of purity, how or why we may not be able to tell. It is impossible to fight directly against self-consciousness. The effort to rid oneself of it by watching against it only roots it more deeply ; but as we strive directly to practise the Presence of God, we find it has brought with it its

twin sister which will not come without it, and
the consciousness of self has melted away in
the light of God's Presence.

Again, many vices spring from virtues unbalanced by some other virtue which develops
the opposite side of the character. One may,
for instance, be all heart and no head, or all
head and no heart; if so, the powers, great and
noble as they are, that belong to heart or head
will fail of producing their proper fruit, for they
are unbalanced and one-sided. There are
virtues that belong to one side of the character
and leave the other untouched, and consequently each needs the other to balance
and correct it. All prayer and no action,
except in the case of very exceptional vocations,
may lead to great self-deceit. All action and
no prayer fritters away the powers of the soul.

Thus the virtues that belong to one side of
the character need those or the other side to

balance them or they cease to be virtues. Consequently the Christian life is always a surprise, for it is ever showing seemingly opposite characteristics. But it will also display what is more beautiful still, single virtues, which are the outcome of the perfect blending of two graces that are seemingly in opposition. The new virtue is the result of these two being blended in perfect proportion; let the proportion be destroyed and the virtue itself is destroyed.

The virtue of Christian patience is the outcome of the perfect blending of gentleness and strength; if these two do not mingle in perfect proportion, it ceases to be patience; if gentleness outweighs strength, patience degenerates into weakness; if strength outweighs gentleness, it crystallises into hardness. Firmness is the blending in perfect proportion of strength of will and clearness of moral judgment; if there be not the latter, or in proportion as it is lacking, firmness will degenerate into obstinacy or scrupulosity ; if strength of will be not in due proportion, then it is not firmness at all, but passes off into insincerity or even hypocrisy.

But once more, there are virtues which are more comprehensive in their character, they are the condition and support of every other virtue ; there are certain Christian graces which, if you have not, you can have none, and which if you have, all others become possible. They represent attitudes of the soul which fit it for the growth of virtue in general.

There are two such especially, without which no one can mature in any Christian grace. One is, as it were, the soil out of which all must grow —charity. Any virtue that has not spread its roots into this, and that does not suck its nourishment from it, is not a Christian grace. ' Though I have the gift of prophecy, and understand all mysteries and all knowledge ; and though I have all faith, so that I could remove mountains, and have not charity, I am nothing; and though I bestow all my goods to feed the poor, and though I give my body to be burned, and have not charity, it profiteth me nothing.'[1] Charity is the soil in which alone Christian virtues can grow, it is the condition of all else ; though it seems the end, it is the beginning, for there is no virtue where it is not.

And there is another, without which no virtue can mature its growth. Perseverance is not merely the crown and stamp of perfection, it must accompany every step in the growth of every grace ; just as the texture of the tree must be woven firm in every stage of its growth, so perseverance has to watch over the growth of each virtue day by day ; every day in which it fails, the graces which are under its care begin to droop and lose their bloom.

[1] 1 Corinthians xiii. 2, 3.

Thus perseverance is not only a virtue in itself, but it is one without whose constant presence and assistance no other virtue can develop one step in its growth. If charity, then, be the soil into which all must spread their roots, perseverance is the cohesive force that gives form and consistency to all over whose development it presides. And thus temptation will often leave all the graces that the soul is trying to form unassailed, and attack the one grace of perseverance; for it knows well that if it can destroy or weaken this, all else must fail with it. We often meet with people with very high aspirations and the beginnings of many graces and with great possibilities, but nothing in them matures, nothing attains its full bloom, for they are lacking in the one grace which is the guardian and protector of all—they have no perseverance.

Now perseverance having so great a work

to do, having to watch over every good thing that the soul would develop, cannot work alone—it has not only to keep everything under its protection, but it must live both in the present and future ; it must look forward, but it must not for a moment forget the present. It knows indeed that many a promising virtue has died because its possessor was living in the future and neglecting it in the present, and virtues are too delicate to grow untended for a day ; and it knows also that many a virtue has been killed because the soul in which it was trying to grow could not look forward and wait and hope, recognising the law of its organic growth and rejoicing, as it saw the blade, in the thought of the full-grown ear.

Therefore perseverance needs the aid of two fellow-workers : it needs, as it were, eyes with which to look forward, and hands with which to toil. It must keep ever before it the ideal towards which it presses, and it must never cease to work towards that ideal. Perseverance is not a mere dogged plodding on toward an unseen end, it is full of inspiration and enthusiasm ; in all its endeavours, therefore, it is assisted by the two fellow-workers, hope and patience.

Natural hope is the spring of all the movement of life, of all activity and progress. Memory links us with the past ; hope looks forward, it is almost creative, as, aided by imagination, it lifts the veil from the future. Men are ready to forego the greatest enjoyments in the present in the desire of what hope promises, but in the midst of their plans let hope die, and their hands fall heavily by their side. As we look at the busy world, with all its competitions and sacrifice, and ask what is the spring that sets it in motion, we answer, *hope* ; the manifold powers of heart and mind and will are developed and unfolded under its inspiration.

And it is the same in the spiritual life; hope here receives a new direction ; it looks to no earthly end, it looks to heaven ; it stimulates men to no mere temporal activities, but to the development of Christian graces, and the preparation for the vision of God ; it sees the end already attained, the prize won, and that vision, as it beams brighter and brighter, kindles the soul with ambitions so great that it is prepared, before it has obtained a single grace except this one, to forego everything for this end. Faith looks backward as well as forward, hope only looks forward. Faith embraces in its vision heaven and hell ; hope cannot see hell, it cannot contemplate failure, it sees what it aims for as already its possession, and then gathers all its forces to succeed.

Thus perseverance is aided and inspired by hope. And patience, the unwearied worker, plods on enlightened and sustained by hope,

never resting, never fainting ; while the eyes of
hope are resting on the far-off vision of attainment, the hands of patience work steadily on to
accomplish its present task. So it was with Peter;
our Lord lifted the veil and showed him the future,
his end the martyr's death. 'When thou shalt
be old, thou shalt stretch forth thy hands, and
another shall gird thee, and carry thee whither
thou wouldest not. This said He, signifying by
what death he should glorify God.' That was
what he was to work towards. 'And when He
had spoken this, He said unto him, Follow
Me.'¹ If that end was to be reached, he must
now be following Christ, he must work for it in
the present.

Thus that work-a-day, commonplace virtue,
perseverance, is full of inspiration. Hope the
idealist, patience the practical plodder, co-
operate to accomplish her task. As days and

¹ S. John xxi. 18, 19.

years go by, and she goes on steadily and un-swervingly with her work, it is not all mere dry, hard plodding ; bright dreams burn before her eyes and kindle her heart, she is all on fire within, though she looks so calm and common-place, for Hope ever stands by her side like a prophet to stimulate and inspire. She works like an artist with the model before her eyes and the chisel and hammer in her hands, and like an artist her heart burns within her as she works.

Perseverance, therefore, may fail in one of two ways, either by losing hope or by losing patience. If hope fail, the work will lose all life and inspiration and will become mechanical ; if patience, it will never be completed.

Thus some persons go on with their religious duties, their prayers and rule, or whatever it may be they have undertaken, but it can easily be seen, after a time, that there is

no heart in what they are doing ; it becomes
more and more mechanical and lifeless, it does
not develop or strengthen the character; it
might as well be given up, perhaps it would
be better to give it up, for there is no effort
to gain anything through what is being done.
Hope has died, there is no looking forward to
the end, and the hands work heavily.

Others, again, begin with enthusiasm, are
borne along for a time by the strength of their
enthusiastic impulse, but at the first failure they
lose patience and give up. They see the end ;
the eye of hope is open and kindles the heart,
but they cannot endure the failures and delays
which come between the vision and its fulfilment. Sometimes they end in becoming mere
dreamers, thinking what one day they will do,
imagining themselves only held back by circumstances, living a life of dreams with their
eyes fixed upon the far-off future and their

hands fallen listlessly by their sides, forgetting that the only way to fulfil their hopes is by present effort.

Thus two different kinds of persons will fail of the grace of perseverance in quite different ways.

But how are such elements of failure to be corrected, for they apparently belong to the very character itself? They can only really be corrected through union with Christ. There may be a natural despondency and a supernatural hope, a natural impulsiveness and a supernatural patience. It is necessary for many that they should learn deeply through failure after failure, that 'they have no power of themselves to help themselves,' before they can learn the meaning of these great words, 'I can do all things through Christ who strengtheneth me.' [1] He who said them had learnt it, for he said

[1] Philippians iv. 13.

again, 'When I am weak, then am I strong.'[1] He
was conscious at the same time of natural weakness and supernatural strength.   He had learnt
through his own incapacity where to find the
power he needed.   There is no necessary connexion between a naturally hopeful and bright
disposition and the Christian grace of hope ; it
is not impossible that these may exist in in-
verse proportion in the same person.   Natural
hopefulness may not be able to stand out
against constant failure in moral and spiritual
things.   The despair that springs from the sense
of one's own weakness, and the breaking down
of resolution after resolution, may be the birth-
pangs of Christian hope.   Only when the soul
has suffered much from many physicians and
finds itself grow nothing the better, but rather
the worse, does it at last come to our Lord.   The
constant sense of failure, the seeming powerless-

[1] 2 Cor. xii. 10.

ness to stand before certain temptations, may be the means of leading one to find a new sense of power. ' All my fresh springs shall be in thee.' [1] Consequently the power of a sustained and un-failing hopefulness by which perseverance may be gained does not depend upon, is, indeed, alto-gether independent of natural disposition ; it is based upon and grows out of spiritual experi-ence. The soul has learnt that in the moment of weakness Christ can strengthen it ; that, in spite of the most rooted habits, it can, in the power of our Lord, withstand old temptations before which once it was powerless. The hope that it has gained is built upon a more sure foundation than any gift of nature ; it is built upon the experienced truth of the promises of Christ.

Thus in the life of the soul that goes plod-ding on and struggling with its faults and temp-

[1] Psalm lxxxvii. 7.

tations there are often to be found two stages :
first, failure and discouragement and a loss of
interest or joy in what it is doing, and, not un-
frequently, the sense of going through one's
duties in a mechanical and lifeless way, and then
there 'springs up a light for the righteous, and
joyful gladness for them who'—in spite of all
failure—'are true of heart ;'[1] and the heart is
refreshed and the will invigorated as the eye
stretches beyond the present and sees the ac-
complished end. Divine hope has come, and all
is changed.

And it is the same with patience ; impulse
wears away and things undertaken in the
excitement of some strong emotion are left
unfinished. The experience of life teaches the
soul that the noblest dreams and the highest
ideals will not be fulfilled by fitful efforts,
however strong and passionate they may be

[1] Psalm xcvii. 11.

while they last, and that great ambitions do not of themselves make one great. At last it learns that what it needs is the disciplined faithfulness, sustained by rule and principle amidst all the fluctuations of feeling. This it gains in Christ ; all the bright dreams of what it hoped to be fade and re-form round another centre, our Lord Himself ; and as the soul tries to approach, it finds that it cannot by impulsive efforts, but only by constant and growing habits of mind and action. It learns that in an hour's reaction after some time of spiritual excitement it may lose more than it gained. It learns that they who would know Christ must be strong and patient, and live on through times of coldness and apparent rejection. Thus it learns the lesson of patience and discipline at the feet of Christ, and as it does, it sees, too, how its ideal becomes transformed, and with hopeful patience it fights its way on to its final triumph in Him. Do we not know such men, who go on quietly and steadily fighting their way through difficulty after difficulty, never giving in to the sense of failure that would bid them give up, and never losing sight of their end; who under the inspiration of hope are protected from becoming mechanical, and under the protection of patience are preserved from the discouragements that beset the pathway of progress, and thus beneath the guardianship of perseverance enrich their souls with many virtues that mature and ripen to perfection.

PRINTED BY
SPOTTISWOODE AND CO., NEW STREET SQUARE
LONDON

www.ingramcontent.com/pod-product-compliance
Lightning Source LLC
Chambersburg PA
CBHW020608030726
47497CB00007B/2145